Proverbs

Real wisdom
for real life

by Kathleen B. Nielson
and Rachel Jones

thegoodbook
COMPANY

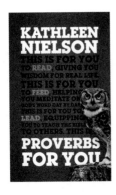

Proverbs For You

These studies are adapted from *Proverbs For You*. If you are reading *Proverbs For You* alongside this Good Book Guide, here is how the studies in this booklet link to the chapters of *Proverbs For You*:

Study One → Ch 1
Study Two → Ch 2-3
Study Three → Ch 4
Study Four → Ch 5

Study Five → Ch 7
Study Six → Ch 10
Study Seven → Ch 12
Study Eight → Ch 13

Find out more about *Proverbs For You* at:
www.thegoodbook.com/for-you

Real wisdom for real life
The Good Book Guide to Proverbs
© Kathleen Nielson/The Good Book Company, 2020
Series Consultants: Tim Chester, Tim Thornborough,
Anne Woodcock, Carl Laferton

Published by:
The Good Book Company

thegoodbook.com | thegoodbook.co.uk
thegoodbook.com.au | thegoodbook.co.nz | thegoodbook.co.in

ISBN: 9781784984304

Printed in Turkey

CONTENTS

Introduction: Good Book Guides

Every Bible-study group is different—yours may take place in a church building, in a home or in a cafe, on a train, over a leisurely mid-morning coffee or squashed into a 30-minute lunch break. Your group may include new Christians, mature Christians, non-Christians, moms and tots, students, businessmen or teens. That's why we've designed these *Good Book Guides* to be flexible for use in many different situations.

Our aim in each session is to uncover the meaning of a passage, and see how it fits into the "big picture" of the Bible. But that can never be the end. We also need to appropriately apply what we have discovered to our lives. Let's take a look at what is included:

⊕ **Talkabout:** Most groups need to "break the ice" at the beginning of a session, and here's the question that will do that. It's designed to get people talking around a subject that will be covered in the course of the Bible study.

⊕ **Investigate:** The Bible text for each session is broken up into manageable chunks, with questions that aim to help you understand what the passage is about. The **Leader's Guide** contains **guidance for questions**, and sometimes ⊗ additional "follow-up" questions.

⊡ **Explore more (optional):** These questions will help you connect what you have learned to other parts of the Bible, so you can begin to fit it all together like a jig-saw; or occasionally look at a part of the passage that's not dealt with in detail in the main study.

⊡ **Apply:** As you go through a Bible study, you'll keep coming across **apply** sections. These are questions to get the group discussing what the Bible teaching means in practice for you and your church. ⊡ **Getting personal** is an opportunity for you to think, plan and pray about the changes that you personally may need to make as a result of what you have learned.

⊕ **Pray:** We want to encourage prayer that is rooted in God's word—in line with his concerns, purposes and promises. So each session ends with an opportunity to review the truths and challenges highlighted by the Bible study, and turn them into prayers of request and thanksgiving.

The **Leader's Guide** and introduction provide historical background information, explanations of the Bible texts for each session, ideas for **optional extra** activities, and guidance on how best to help people uncover the truths of God's word.

Why study Proverbs?

Human beings are and always have been in need of wisdom. Wisdom helps us make decisions about what work to do; what to say (or not say); what person to marry (or avoid). Wisdom points us to habits that tend to make life smoother and happier. Wisdom gives shape and meaning to our cries of both suffering and delight. In general, wisdom offers insight into the concrete experiences of human life. That's the commonly understood sense of wisdom.

But Proverbs offers God-breathed wisdom. This wisdom is utterly recognizable in that (like popular wisdom) it offers insight into the concrete experiences of human life. But it's also utterly different because it offers godly insight into the concrete experiences of human life in a world created and ruled by the Lord God of the Scriptures.

Proverbs addresses the spectrum of human activities and concerns that make up daily life: from eating and drinking to the way we speak to one another, to family and social relationships, to sex, to business dealings, and on and on. Proverbs calls us to see all the experiences of our lives in relation to the Lord, who created and rules the world, who calls us first to fear him, and who himself shows us how to live wisely.

Rather than taking a more thematic approach, we'll approach the book of Proverbs as God has given it to us—a carefully shaped poetic book that holds together as a piece of literature from beginning to end.

In just eight studies we can only begin to take account of Proverbs' wealth of insights. But let's begin. Let's see how the first nine chapters establish a foundation for all that follows—a foundation that keeps reappearing and even deepening at crucial points in the book. Let's taste the flavors of the various proverb collections built on that foundation, and let's hear the themes develop and wind around one another—kind of as they do in a day of real life! And let's allow these proverbs to point us to the source of wisdom: Jesus Christ, in whom "are hidden all the treasures of wisdom and knowledge" (Colossians 2:3).

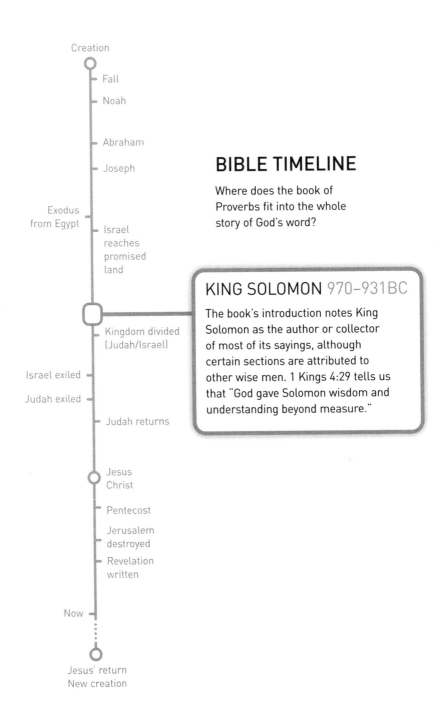

Creation

Fall

Noah

Abraham

Joseph

Exodus from Egypt

Israel reaches promised land

BIBLE TIMELINE

Where does the book of Proverbs fit into the whole story of God's word?

KING SOLOMON 970–931BC

The book's introduction notes King Solomon as the author or collector of most of its sayings, although certain sections are attributed to other wise men. 1 Kings 4:29 tells us that "God gave Solomon wisdom and understanding beyond measure."

Kingdom divided (Judah/Israel)

Israel exiled

Judah exiled

Judah returns

Jesus Christ

Pentecost

Jerusalem destroyed

Revelation written

Now

Jesus' return
New creation

1

THE BEGINNING OF WISDOM

⊕ talkabout

1. In our culture, what different "voices" offer wisdom on how to live well?

• How do you decide who to listen to?

⊥ investigate

Whether it's books on business, podcasts on parenting, or articles on the art of home décor—we humans desperately reach out for wisdom.

Centuries ago, God's people living in the kingdom of Israel also knew this universal need for wisdom. The nations surrounding them—Egypt, Arabia, Babylon, Phoenicia—had their own voices offering insight into the concrete experiences of human life. Proverbs is similar in style and approach to this other wisdom literature, but fundamentally different in its nature and source—as the book's "prologue" (1:1-7) makes clear.

▶ Read Proverbs 1:1

2. Who is the book of Proverbs attributed to? What made his wisdom different from that of the nations around him? (See 1 Kings 4:29.)

• What does verse 1 tell us about where Proverbs fits into the bigger story of God's people in the Old Testament?

⊡ explore more

optional

"Wisdom" in Solomon's day was not a new or foreign concept for the Israelites; in fact, wisdom had always been connected to God and to his revealed word.

❯ Read Deuteronomy 4:5-8

Deuteronomy is Moses' sermon to the Israelites as they prepared to enter the promised land (around 450 years before Solomon).

What does Moses say the people need to do in order to be wise?

Why did God intend for the Israelites to be wiser than the nations around them?

Think forward in Bible history through the Old Testament. Did Israel ultimately succeed or fail in this task, do you think?

Think forward in Bible history to the New Testament. How did Jesus fulfill what Israel failed to do?

❯ Read Proverbs 1:2-6

3. Verses 2-4 lay out the book's aim. What will Proverbs equip the hearer to do?

• Verse 2

DICTIONARY

Righteousness (v 3): right judgements and actions.
Equity (v 3): fairness.
Prudence (v 4): carefulness.
Discretion (v 4): showing good judgement.

- Verse 3

- Verse 4

4. What do these different ideas tell you about the nature of wisdom?

It's helpful to think of wisdom in this book as a kaleidoscope of patterns. As Proverbs asks us to consider wisdom, it does not present a neat list of truths to learn and affirm. Rather, Proverbs points to wisdom that transforms all of life.

5. What do verses 5-6...
- call us to do?

- promise as a reward?

6. Who is the book's wisdom addressed to (v 4, 5)?

⊡ apply

It's thought that this book was originally used for Israel's leaders-in-training. Yet Proverbs' wisdom is continually needed by all of us, young and old, male and female. You are included in the ones who need to stop and listen (v 5)!

7. Proverbs warns against ever thinking we've outgrown the need to seek wisdom. How can we tell if we're in danger of having that attitude?

- What does it look like to continue to stop, listen, and learn as we grow in Christian maturity?

⊡ getting personal

Jesus likewise taught that wisdom lies in hearing and doing God's word: "Everyone then who hears these words of mine and does them will be like a wise man who built his house on the rock" (Matthew 7:24). Is there an area of your life where you need to observe this challenge to "hear" and "do" this week?

⊡ investigate

▶ **Read Proverbs 1:7**

DICTIONARY

LORD (v 6): the personal covenant name for God.

8. What "opposites" does this verse set up?

9. What does it mean to fear the Lord, do you think?

⊡ getting personal

"The fear of the LORD is the beginning of knowledge." To what extent is your spiritual life marked with this kind of deep reverence? How, practically, can you seek to grow in this fear?

Proverbs' wisdom is found in relationship with the Lord. Yet we read the book of Proverbs today knowing that the kingdom of Israel (Proverbs 1:1) flourished and then fell, as God's people turned away from their Lord. Only a remnant faithfully believed God's word and trusted God's promises of forgiveness and redemption.

The fulfillment of God's promises to them arrived in the deliverer who came from the line of King David—the Lord Jesus. He is the One in whom are hidden all the treasures of wisdom and knowledge (Colossians 2:3); he is the One who makes relationship with the Lord possible.

People choosing the path of folly don't need just an argument; they need to meet a person.

10. **Read 1 Corinthians 1:18-25.** How does Jesus, "the wisdom of God" (v 24), bring about our salvation? What else strikes you from these verses?

⮕ apply

11. In what areas of your life do you most feel in need of wisdom? What would it look like to fear the Lord in these circumstances?

12. "People choosing the path of folly don't need just an argument; they need to meet a person." How have you seen that to be true in your own experience?

- How should that shape the way you seek to speak wisdom into the lives of others (both Christians and non-Christians)?

⬆ pray

Spend time praising God for Christ: the power of God and the wisdom of God.

Pray for his help to fear him rightly as you walk in reverent relationship with him day by day.

Then pray through Proverbs 1:2-6, asking that you would indeed grow in each of these qualities as you study the book of Proverbs.

2 Proverbs 1:8 – 7:27
TWO PATHS

⊕ talkabout

1. What is some of the best advice you received as a child, from parents or teachers?

⊕ investigate

After the prologue, in chapters 1 – 9 we find ten "instructions" that begin with "My son." The instructions are interspersed with several "wisdom sections." These first nine chapters establish a foundation of wisdom, beginning with the fear of the Lord. In this study, we'll take a look at the first instruction (1:8-19) and the first wisdom section (1:20-33).

❯ Read Proverbs 1:8-19

> **DICTIONARY**
>
> **Sheol (v 12):** the place of the dead.

2. What is the son called to do, and what is the reward for doing that (v 8-9)?

• What is the alternative to hearing (suggested in v 8b)?

3. What instruction does the father give to his son? ("Do not..." v 10, 15)

* And why? ("For..." v 16-19)

We'll continue to see this image of two paths—those of wisdom and folly—throughout the book of Proverbs.

⮕ apply

4. At its most basic level, this instruction warns youths against joining gangs of looters! What other, broader applications does the passage suggest to us?

⭳ investigate

Next we come to the first of the "wisdom sections." Here, wisdom is pictured as a woman.

▶ Read Proverbs 1:20-33

5. What is Wisdom doing, and where (v 20-21)?

* Who is she speaking to, and what does she long for them to do (v 22-23)?

6. What do the following verses tell us about the possible responses to Wisdom, and the consequences of them?

• Verses 24-28

• Verses 29-31

• Verses 32-33

This woman brings us a living picture of the very words of God. Often she sounds like one of God's prophets. Indeed, when she speaks, it sounds a lot like God speaking! This poetic picture is intended to enliven our imaginations and hearts to hear the very voice of God in his revelation to us.

7. Look again at this picture of Wisdom. What does she show us about God?

⌨ **explore more**

optional

Look up some of the following passages and compare them to Proverbs 1:20-33. How does Wisdom echo God's word in these other parts of Scripture?
   • Jeremiah 4:14 and Numbers 14:11, 27
   • Joel 2:28-29 and Acts 2:17
   • Psalm 2:4

⊌ investigate

The big point of Proverbs 1 was this: to find wisdom we must begin with the fear of the Lord—which involves listening to his word. That point is now further developed across the next six chapters.

Choose two of the remaining nine instruction sections, and use questions 8 and 9 to guide you through them.

- Instruction 2 (2:1-22)
- Instruction 3 (3:1-12)
- Instruction 4 (3:21-35)
- Instruction 5 (4:1-9)
- Instruction 6 (4:10-19)
- Instruction 7 (4:20-27)
- Instruction 8 (5:1-23)
- Instruction 9 (6:20-35)
- Instruction 10 (7:1-27)

The remaining "wisdom sections" are 3:13-20 and 6:1-19, as well as 8:1-36 and 9:1-18, which we will look at in study 3.

8. *First instruction of your choice:* What is the structure of this instruction? (Hint: Look for repeated refrains, and for linking words like "if," "then," "for," "so," "because," and "therefore.")

- What is the key idea of this instruction?

• How are the two paths—wisdom and folly—made vivid in this passage?

9. *Second instruction of your choice:* What is the structure of this instruction?

• What is the key idea of this instruction?

• How are the two paths—wisdom and folly—made vivid in this passage?

🎲 explore more

The wisdom section in chapter 3 is one of Proverbs' most lovely (and important) passages. It's been called a "hymn to wisdom" because the poetry sings the blessings of those who find it—or rather, her. The best way to get into this poem about wisdom is to read it out loud multiple times and take time to relish it.

❯ Read Proverbs 3:13-20

What are wisdom's value (v 14-15) and benefits (v 16-18)?

What other parts of the Bible are you reminded of as you read this poem? How does it turn your thoughts to the Lord Jesus?

➔ apply

10. Has there been a time when God's word called you from the path of folly, or a time when you were able to give a call to someone heading down that path?

11. In what ways have you have experienced the blessings of walking the path of wisdom, fearing the Lord?

⊡ getting personal

Choose one image, idea, promise, or warning from this study that you particularly want to hold on to. How will you do that this week?

⬆ pray

Praise God for the times when he has mercifully called you back from the path of folly.

Thank God for the blessings that you've experienced as you've sought to walk the path of wisdom—blessings fully given in Christ, through his word, by his Spirit.

Ask for God's help to choose wisdom over folly in the choices—big and small—that you will face this week.

3

Proverbs 8:1 – 9:18
WOMEN CALLING

⊕ talkabout

1. Have you ever been duped into buying a cheap imitation of the real deal? How did it work out, and how did you feel?

Proverbs' opening section (chapters 1 – 9) ends as it has progressed: with voices calling. One offers life; the other offers a deadly imitation.

⊕ investigate

Chapter 7 puts a seductive adulteress before our eyes and ears. Then, in the fourth and climactic wisdom section in chapter 8, we again hear Wisdom call. It's as if she is lifting her veil, revealing herself more and more clearly—and we can only marvel at what we get to see.

❯ Read Proverbs 8:1-36

2. What do we learn about Wisdom's…

- words (v 4-11)?

> **DICTIONARY**
>
> **An abomination (v 7):** disgusting, offensive.
> **Blessed (v 32, 34):** happy; given good things by God.

- benefits (v 12-21)?

In verses 22-31, the speech rises to its most exalted point, as Wisdom reveals her identity as one who has been with God from before creation and in the very process of creation.

3. What is the overall mood of verses 22-31?

- How do these words point us forward to what the New Testament reveals about Christ? (See John 1:1-3; Colossians 1:15-17 and 2:3.)

4. How do the concluding verses (v 32-36) remind us of the two paths pictured throughout Proverbs?

⤷ apply

5. Do you tend to associate wisdom (living God's way) with the kind of joy and delight we see in chapter 8 or with something more dour? Why might that be, do you think? How can we keep the breathtaking goodness of God's wisdom in view?

☺ getting personal

"Does not wisdom call? Does not understanding raise her voice? ... Blessed is the one who listens to me" (Proverbs 8:1, 34). The wonderful truth is that God's words keep mercifully calling us, sinful and simple as we human beings are. How does chapter 8 move you to humility and to gratitude?

⬇ investigate

With all these voices calling, it's clear that we must respond. That's what the final chapter of this section asks us to do. We see two directly contrasting figures at either end of Proverbs 9—Wisdom (v 1-6) and Folly (v 13-18)—with wise instruction in between (v 7-12).

❯ Read Proverbs 9:1-18

6. Compare the woman Wisdom (v 1-6) with the woman Folly (v 7-12).

• What similarities do you see?

• What are the differences?

⬊ explore more

optional

The theme of feasting in the presence of the Lord is one which resonates throughout Scripture. Read one or more of the following passages. How do they echo the themes we see in Proverbs 9:1-6?

❯ Read Exodus 24:9-11; Isaiah 25:6; John 6:35, 50-51; Revelation 19:6-9

7. What, according to verse 10, is the key to choosing Wisdom over Folly?

8. What else marks the wise from the foolish (v 7-9)?

9. Proverbs 9:10 serves as a bookend with the same statement in the prologue (1:7). What have we learned about living in the fear of the Lord since then?

⊡ **getting personal**

Think about a recent time when you received correction. What does your response reveal about your relative wisdom or folly? When do you expect to receive correction in the future, and how will you aim to respond wisely?

→ **apply**

10. How do you experience the conflicting voices of Wisdom and Folly calling in your everyday life? In what ways do they make similar offers but with very different consequences?

11. How can we get better at being the kind of people who rightly give and receive wise correction?

⊼ **pray**

Use Proverbs 8:22-31 to fuel your praise of the Lord Jesus, before asking for God's help to discern the difference between wisdom and folly.

4 Proverbs 10:1-32
INTO THE SWIRL

⊕ talkabout

1. What are some of your favorite poems or song lyrics? What is it about the words that makes them so powerful?

⊥ investigate

We've arrived at Proverbs 10, where the collection of "the proverbs of Solomon" begins. Proverbs are short, pithy, easy-to-remember sayings. People sometimes say that a proverb is like wisdom in a nutshell.

The book of Proverbs consists completely of poetry; the proverbs "proper" (beginning in chapter 10) are especially condensed poetry. Before we begin reading, it's helpful to think through two main characteristics of Proverbs' poetry: imagery and parallelism.

Imagery is picture language which makes us stop and imagine (e.g. 11:22). Parallelism refers to the balancing together of parallel ideas, most often in what we see as two parallel lines. For example, in 1:8 the corresponding parts are easily discernible: "hear" and "forsake not"; "your father's" and "your mother's"; "instruction" and "teaching." Sometimes the two parallel lines say almost the same thing (synonymous parallelism), but often with the second line developing the idea (e.g. 22:24) or making it more vivid (e.g. 16:18). Sometimes the two parallel lines say opposite sorts of things (antithetic parallelism) (e.g. 15:1). But the parallel lines are never exactly opposite or exactly matching. So when examining Proverbs' couplets, it's a good idea to look for surprises. Many different kinds of parallelism exist; the important thing is to notice how the units of meaning balance each other as they speak to us.

This poetry seeps into our minds and hearts as we "chew" on it. The proverbs are a bit like hard candy: if you bite down fast, you just break your teeth, but if you suck on it slowly, the flavor unfolds.

❯ Read Proverbs 10:1-5

DICTIONARY

Slack (v 4): lazy.
Diligent (v 4): hard
and careful worker.

2. What themes from Proverbs 1 – 9 do you see repeated here?

3. Look at verses 1, 4, and 5. What opposite ideas are held up as contrasts (antithetic parallelism)?

4. If you only had the first line of the following verses in front of you, how might you expect the second line to go?

    • Verse 2

    • Verse 3

5. What is surprising about what the second line actually says, and what does that teach us?

    • Verse 2

• Verse 3

:-) **getting personal**

"Righteousness delivers from death" (Proverbs 10:2).

In the full light of Scripture, we know that only one man has ever lived a completely righteous life: Jesus Christ, the Son of God. He received God's full rewards, and believers receive those rewards in him. The "righteous" in Old Testament times looked ahead in faith to this righteous One, who would come to save, offering himself as the perfect sacrifice for the sins for all who believe (Romans 3:21-22; 4:3). Pause to thank Jesus that his righteousness delivers you from death.

> **Read Proverbs 10:6-32**

6. How many different themes or situations does this chapter speak into? List as many as you can.

<table>
<tr><td>DICTIONARY</td></tr>
<tr><td>Transgression (v 19): sin.
Tempest (v 25): storm.</td></tr>
</table>

• Why did God give us the Proverbs in such a diverse swirl, rather than grouped by theme, do you think?

Proverbs 10:6 begins a scattered but discernible cluster of proverbs in this chapter, relating to words and the tongue. There are some challenges that we don't encounter immediately when we get up in the morning—but controlling our tongue is not one of them. So here it is, right away!

7. What different things does this chapter say about our words? What images and patterns do you notice?
   - Verse 6
   - Verse 8
   - Verse 10
   - Verse 11
   - Verse 18
   - Verse 19
   - Verse 20
   - Verse 32

8. Where do our words come from, according to these proverbs?

   - What does this suggest about how we can become less foolish with our words? What will (and what won't) "work"?

☺ **getting personal**

Can you remember a time when you said something you wish you had not said? What was going on in your heart at the time? In what situations will you need to watch your tongue (and your heart) this week?

⊡ explore more

Let's look at what the New Testament says about our words.

▸ Read James 3:1-12

How does this passage reiterate what we've seen in Proverbs 10? What extra layers of meaning does it offer?

▸ Read John 4:13-14

How does Jesus solve the problem of our "salty spring"?

⊖ apply

9. How is Proverbs 10's wisdom on words different from the way in which the world normally encourages us to use words?

10. How have you seen the truth of Proverbs' teaching on words play out in your experience, both positively and negatively?

11. Pick any one proverb from Proverbs 10 that you'd like to "chew" on this week. Why that one?

⬆ **pray**

Praise God for this incredible book, which speaks into the swirl of our everyday lives.

Ask him to transform your heart so that you might use your words wisely.

5 Proverbs 14:1 – 16:9
THE LORD AT THE CENTER

⊕ talkabout

1. "There is no black and white—there are only shades of gray." So goes a popular saying. From what you've read so far, would the writer of Proverbs agree? What makes you say that?

⊥ investigate

▶ Read Proverbs 14:1 – 15:33

2. How does 14:1 picture the two ways of wisdom and folly?

• How does verse 2 describe the two ways? What is the crux of the difference?

Throughout Proverbs, we observe this direct contrast: wisdom vs. folly. And this fundamental attitude is manifested in the way one "walks" or lives: in honest dealings vs. dishonest ones, truthful words vs. lies, and so forth. The examples continue in these chapters, with folly showing more and more of its colors.

3. What do the two ways look like in terms of a person's reactions? (14:16-19, 29; 15:18)

4. What do the two ways look like in terms of a person's attitude to the poor (14:20-21, 31), and to wealth in general (15:16-17, 25)?

• Why is it wrong to oppress the poor?

How does this principle translate for Christians today? (See, for example, 2 Corinthians 9:6-15.)

5. The two ways are not always easily discernible. Sometimes folly can masquerade as wisdom. Consider the following verses. How does the thing that appears better actually turn out to not be better at all?

• 14:4

• 15:17

• Can you think of other examples, from your own life, where following wisdom's path looked worse on the surface but actually turned out to be better?

If we are not the prudent ones who discern beyond appearances (14:15), we will be deceived not just in little, temporary things but also in the ultimate matter of life and death (14:12).

The third key theme in this section is the heart. This word basically describes the inner person, including not simply our emotions but also the core of our whole being.

6. What do these proverbs say about the heart (14:10, 13; 15:11, 13)? How do these verses ring true in your experience?

➔ apply

7. Think about the different themes we've seen so far. How does what you've read challenge the way you think about yourself, other people, and the Lord?

• Anger

• Wealth and justice

• The heart

⭳ investigate

Chapters 14 and 15 have been piling up references to Yahweh, the LORD; they build to a dramatic point of promise/warning in 15:30-33: "The fear of the LORD is instruction in wisdom, and humility comes before honor" (15:33). With that, the stage is set for 16:1-9. This section, moving from the last verses of chapter 15 into the first verses of 16, is described by one commentator as a "theological seam in the middle" of Solomon's proverbs (Lindsay Wilson, *Proverbs*, p 22).

▶ **Read Proverbs 16:1-9**

8. Find the one command in these verses. What does this mean, do you think?

DICTIONARY

Atoned for (v 6): make relationship possible again.

• Why can we have confidence as we do that, according to verses 1-2? (See also verse 9.)

9. What do verses 4-6 tell us about the problem of sin, and its solution?

10. What are the blessings that come from a righteous life (that is, a life lived in the fear of the Lord) (v 7-9)?

⊡ explore more

In Acts 4 we get a helpful picture of what it looks like to live with a "Proverbs 16:1-9" attitude. In the first part of the chapter, Peter and John are arrested by the Jewish council for preaching about Jesus. In the second half the chapter, we see how the church responds…

▶ Read Acts 4:23-31

How do these believers show us what it looks like to live out the truths of Proverbs 16:1-9?

⊡ getting personal

What does it mean, in your circumstances, to "commit your work to the LORD"? What stops you from doing that? Take a moment to pray about that now.

⊖ apply

11. What truths about the Lord in Proverbs 16:1-9 give you comfort and joy? How do those truths point you to Christ?

12. Was there a particular time when you learned more of what it means that our hearts make our plans, but the Lord establishes our steps?

- How does that give you confidence as you look ahead to particular challenges you face in the future?

⬆ pray

Shape your prayers around the "gospel train of thought" we find in Proverbs 16:1-9:

- Declare your trust in the sovereign Lord God (v 1-3).

- Confess your sin and arrogance, and the punishment it deserves (v 4-5).

- Rejoice that through the Lord's steadfast love and faithfulness our iniquity has been atoned for, finally through the death and resurrection of Christ (v 6).

- Ask for God's help to walk in relationship with him as you commit all your ways to him (v 7-9).

6 Proverbs 22:17 – 24:22
THIRTY SAYINGS OF THE WISE

⊕ talkabout

1. Think about some of the ads or commercials you've seen recently. What do they tell you about the kinds of things that people most desire?

Proverbs 22:17 introduces us to a new collection of proverbs: "The Words of the Wise." Many of these proverbs are closely related to an earlier Egyptian wisdom collection titled "Instructions of Amenemope"; evidence suggests that they were borrowed and then adapted to ground this wisdom in its one true source. The purpose of this collection of "thirty sayings" (v 20) is that "your trust may be in the LORD" (v 19).

⊡ explore more

optional

What should we make of the fact that these inspired writings overlap with secular ones? In one sense it should make us even more mindful of the one source of truth: the Lord, who is the Maker of us all. We know that Solomon was able to discuss wisdom with non-Israelites in the ancient world—as he did, for instance, with the queen of Sheba, who heard of Solomon's wisdom and paid him a visit.

▶ **Read 1 Kings 10:1-10**

How did the queen of Sheba respond to Solomon's wisdom? What did she recognize about Solomon (v 9)?

1 Kings 4:29-30 tells us that the wisdom God gave Solomon surpassed the wisdom of all the people of the east and all the wisdom of Egypt. Such comparisons imply not only difference but similarity; the nations around recognized wisdom, although only in a limited way because they did not know the source.

Think about some of the wisdom that we've seen so far in Proverbs. How could you use that to connect with non-Christians you know, while pointing them to the source of true wisdom?

⊕ investigate

▶ Read Proverbs 22:17 – 23:11

DICTIONARY

After the opening call (22:17-21) comes a section of varied proverbs that send the son (and us) out into the world to interact wisely with all kinds of people—especially the rich and poor.

Ancient landmark (22:28; 23:10): probably marked the boundaries of peoples' land.

2. Look at 22:22-23 and 23:10-11. How should the wise treat the poor, and why?

Redeemer (23:11): an Old Testament title for God, meaning someone who restores another.

23:1-9 pictures two deceptive dinner parties.

3. Why is the son warned to watch out...
   • in the house of the ruler (v 1-3)?

   • in the house of the stingy man (v 6-9)?

4. Between these two dinner scenes is the key lesson to be learned. What is it (v 4-5)?

• Why is toiling to acquire wealth foolish (v 5)?

⊖ apply

5. Elsewhere Proverbs speaks of wealth as the reward of hard work, and warns that laziness leads to poverty. What are some differences between working hard to make a living and toiling to acquire wealth? How can we tell if we are being unwise in this area?

6. Who are the poor or defenseless near you, whose cause you could plead? How could you seek to light up their lives with God's justice and mercy?

⊙ investigate

▶ **Read Proverbs 23:12-35**

7. What do these verses say about...
• how parents should relate to their children?

• how children should relate to their parents?

8. What two specific evils does the father warn his son against (v 19-21, 29-35)?

- What do these things have in common? What makes them so dangerous? And how do these verses powerfully communicate the danger?

▶ **Read Proverbs 24:1-22**

Verses 1-2 and verses 19-22 work as a pair of bookends; both units call the listener not to envy the wicked or desire to join them.

9. Looking at the verses in between (v 3-18), why do you think wisdom is much more desirable instead?

10. What hope do these verses offer for when we encounter hard times (v 5, 10, 16)?

- How will wise people respond when others encounter difficulties (v 17-18)?

⊡ getting personal

It's a good test of our souls to ask what we really desire, deep down. Where do our thoughts go when we wake up in the middle of the night or when we first wake up in the morning? What kind of desire motivates us to work or serve or exercise or diet—what are we after? Do we hunger for God's word? Does it fill our minds regularly?

Wisdom's house is a house we must want to live in. By putting this vivid portrait in front of us, Proverbs helps us to desire the Lord's way and to seek after the Lord Jesus, who is our wisdom from God.

⊟ apply

11. In what areas have the thirty sayings of the wise shown your desires to be out of kilter?

12. We live in a world that encourages us to desire so much other than wisdom! As a community of believers, how can we help one another to remember that the Lord's wisdom is our ultimate source of goodness and strength?

⬆ pray

Spend some time praying in light of your answers to question 11. Ask God to give you a greater desire for the goodness and strength of his wisdom, given to us fully in Christ.

You could finish your prayer time by saying or singing the words of this hymn:

Be thou my vision, O Lord of my heart;
Naught be all else to me, save that thou art.
Thou my best thought, by day or by night,
Waking or sleeping, thy presence my light.

Be thou my Wisdom, and thou my true Word;
I ever with thee and thou with me, Lord;
Thou my great Father, I thy true son;
Thou in me dwelling, and I with thee one.

Be thou my battle shield, sword for the fight;
Be thou my dignity, thou my delight;
Thou my soul's shelter, thou my high tow'r:
Raise thou me heav'nward, O pow'r of my pow'r.

Riches I heed not, nor man's empty praise,
Thou mine Inheritance, now and always:
Thou and thou only, first in my heart,
High King of heaven, my treasure thou art.

(Translated by Eleanor Hull, 1912)

7 Proverbs 30:1-33
A HUMBLE HEART

⊕ talkabout

1. Most of us have a long list of prayer requests that we regularly pray about. But imagine you could only ask God for two things. What would they be, and why?

⊕ investigate

In Proverbs 30 we meet the mysterious figure of Agur. We don't know who he is, but we do know that he speaks an "oracle" (30:1)—that is, words from God. Agur's words give us the book's most personal account of what it's like to live out the fear of the Lord.

❱ Read Proverbs 30:1-9

2. We're nearing the end of a book that is intended to help us to "know wisdom" (1:1). What, then, is surprising about Agur's words in 30:1-3?

> **DICTIONARY**
>
> **Oracle (v 1):** words inspired by God.

- Read Proverbs 26:12. What is not surprising about Agur's attitude?

3. What are the answers to Agur's questions in verse 4, humanly speaking?

• What other answer could we give to those questions?

☺ **explore more**

optional

> ▶ Read Job 38:1-11; 40:3-5

What similarities do you see between Proverbs 30:4 and Job 38:1-11? How does Job model a wise response to God's creative might (40:3-5)?

After setting our own small store of human wisdom in perspective, Agur looks up and celebrates the God who gives wisdom to us, in his word.

4. Look at verse 5. Why are both halves of this verse important, and wonderful?

5. Sum up what "two things" Agur asks God for in verses 7-9.

6. What do Agur's prayer requests reveal about his attitude?

⊡ apply

7. Compare Agur's prayer requests with your answer to question 1. What might you need to learn from him?

- How might your prayer times as a group sound different if you were to take a leaf out of Agur's book?

⊡ investigate

In the chapter's second part it feels as if Agur gets up from his prayers and goes outside. Here is an opportunity to observe the world through the eyes of a wise man with a humble heart.

These verses are arranged into six lists of "fours," interspersed with three warnings (v 10, v 17, v 32-33). They represent an ability to order and pattern reality, rather than simply to be buffeted by the swirl. This ability reflects the image of God our Creator, who in the beginning brought original order out of chaos—from the planets and stars all numbered and placed to the smallest living creatures in the sea and on the land.

▶ **Read Proverbs 30:10-17**

8. What do these proverbs have to say about humility, self-exaltation, and grasping for more?

Verses 10-17 paint some ugly pictures. But Agur also has eyes for wonderful things…

> **Read Proverbs 30:18-33**

DICTIONARY

9. What is the common thread that ties together each of these "fours"? What is being celebrated or condemned?

    Curds (v 33): the basis of cheese, or butter.

    • Verses 18-19, and 20 (Clue: It's about boundaries.)

    • Verses 21-23 (Clue: It's about overreaching.)

    • Verses 24-28 (Clue: It's about living *with the grain*.)

    • Verses 29-31 (Clue: It's about confidence.)

10. In what sense do verses 32-33 sum up the message of chapter 30?

• What is the alternative to "exalting yourself" (v 32), according to Proverbs?

⊡ getting personal

Is there an area of your life where you are fighting the temptation to grasp for more? How does Proverbs 30 both challenge and help you? What needs to change in your words, actions, or attitude this week?

⊡ apply

11. How does the culture around us encourage us not to be humble and lowly?

• How might our church culture encourage us not to be humble?

▶ **Read Philippians 2:1-10**

12. How does Jesus show us the way of humility, which leads to honor (v 6-11)? How does he enable us to follow him in that way?

• What should humility look like in our treatment of others (v 1-5)?

⬆ **pray**

Two things I ask of you;
    deny them not to me before I die:
Remove far from me falsehood and lying;
    give me neither poverty nor riches;
feed me with the food that is needful for me,
    lest I be full and deny you
and say, "Who is the LORD?"
    or lest I be poor and steal
and profane the name of my God.

(Proverbs 30:7-9)

Read these verses slowly, pausing line by line to add your own intercessions as you ask God to clean you and feed you.

8 Proverbs 31:1-31
WISDOM LIVED

⊕ talkabout

1. Imagine that a young unmarried man at your church asked you, "What should I look for in a wife?" How would you answer?

The "Proverbs 31 woman" is an answer to that question—a portrait of the kind of wife the "son," who has been listening to the wisdom of proverbs, should seek. But it's also a final picture of wisdom in action, from which we can all learn. Here, in the book's epilogue, Proverbs will send us out in the same way it called us in: by telling us to seek true wisdom—the wisdom that begins and ends with the fear of the Lord.

But first, some wise words from a king…

⊕ investigate

> **Read Proverbs 31:1-9**

Here are the words of a mother to her son on how to be king. How lovely to see, here at the end of Proverbs, a son who listened and learned!

2. What are kings called to do?

• What behavior is not fitting for a king, and why?

King Lemuel's mother did not know she was describing the promised king to come in the line of David. But for believers today, as we read the weighty task of the kingly calling (v 8-9), our minds can't help but be drawn to the Lord Jesus.

3. How did Jesus fulfill the kingly calling in Proverbs 31:8-9? (See also Luke 7:22 and Isaiah 11:1-4.)

⊡ getting personal

This is a passage that leaves us leaning forward to find the true King, even in the midst of sinful ones who need to learn to control their appetites for women and wine. What do you most long for about King Jesus' eternal rule? Take heart. He has come, and he is coming again.

⊕ investigate

▶ Read Proverbs 31:10-31

These verses are an acrostic poem: the twenty-two verses begin consecutively with the twenty-two letters of the Hebrew alphabet. An acrostic poem by its very nature tends to jump from one idea to another, rather than having a clear, logical development. The poem does hold together, however, as a climactic portrait of wisdom in action.

DICTIONARY

Flax (v 13): plant used to make linen.
Maidens (v 15): female servants.
Distaff/spindle (v 19): tools used for making wool into yarn.

4. How do verses 10-12 and 28-31 provide a framework for the poem?

• Stand back and look at the big picture. What kind of words would you use to describe this woman?

5. What kinds of work does she do, and in what manner?

6. How does this woman relate to…

- her husband? (Note the three "husband verses" that hold the poem together.)

- her household?

- her community?

- her God?

7. As the book's concluding piece, this poem draws together the themes of wisdom that we have seen throughout. For example, how do verses 10-11 specifically echo 3:13-14?

• How does verse 26 resonate with what we've seen elsewhere in Proverbs?

8. Climactically, in conclusion to the book, this woman "fears the LORD" (v 30). What is she *not* afraid of, and why (v 21, 25)?

☺ getting personal

As you think about the future, are you fearful or confident (or somewhere in between)? How might growing in the fear of the Lord enable you to laugh "at the time to come"? What or who will help you to do that more this week?

☺ explore more

optional

The Hebrew phrase translated "excellent wife" is *eshet hayil*, or "valiant woman." In some Hebrew Old Testament manuscripts, the book of Ruth follows the book of Proverbs. Proverbs 31's poem, then, would lead directly into a named, historical example of an *eshet hayil*—and that's the exact phrase Boaz uses to describe Ruth in Ruth 3:11.

▶ Read Ruth 3:1-13

Think about what you know about Ruth from the book as a whole. What has she done that makes her an eshet hayil? What does she have in common with the Proverbs 31 woman?
In what ways is her situation different from that of the Proverbs 31 woman?
How does this encourage you, as you seek to live out wisdom's strength in your own situation?

⊡ apply

Does this portrait of all this work seem unrealistic (not to mention exhausting)? In one sense it is. We are not likely to run into any woman who is presently doing all the things listed in this poem. Yet perhaps you've had the experience of attending a funeral for an older saint, reading the obituary, and thinking, "Wow! I had no idea this woman/man did all these things!" The summaries of lifetimes of faithful work are truly impressive—even though day-to-day faithfulness often looks very ordinary. The Proverbs 31 woman is meant to spur us on in a similar way. This is the kind of lived-out wisdom we should seek. It is a life that brings great fruit and eternal blessing (v 28-31).

9. Who do you know who embodies this Proverbs 31 wisdom? How do they spur you on to seek to live out wisdom?

10. How might this poem help you praise the Lord for "the depth of the riches and wisdom and knowledge of God" (Romans 11:33), all made known to us in Christ?

We cannot end the book of Proverbs without acknowledging again that the fullness of wisdom has been ultimately revealed to us in Christ, our wisdom from God (1 Corinthians 1:24). He is the one who came, who died, and who rose again to make it possible for us to live in relationship with the Lord. The life of wisdom shown to us in Proverbs is finally and fully a life lived in Christ—with his word and his Spirit lighting up all the concrete experiences of our everyday lives.

We live in Christ not as individuals but as his body, the church—his bride (Ephesians 5:22-33; Revelation 19:6-9). Even though the writers of Proverbs did not know the full story of redemption, they pictured a wife as the final portrait of wisdom lived out. Beautiful resonances emerge when we read Proverbs 31 with the full light of the gospel shining back on it, showing us this bride in action. There is much grace in the truth that we believers live out this high calling not individually but all together, for the glory of our Savior.

11. How does Proverbs 31 excite you about living together as God's people in Christ?

12. Look back over the previous studies. What has most thrilled, challenged, or encouraged you from your time in the book of Proverbs?

⬆ pray

Spend time praying for yourselves and for your church family—that you would live out wisdom in the fear of the Lord.

Proverbs

LEADER'S GUIDE

Leader's Guide

INTRODUCTION

Leading a Bible study can be a bit like herding cats—everyone has a different idea of what the passage could be about, and a different line of enquiry that they want to pursue. But a good group leader is more than someone who just referees this kind of discussion. You will want to:

• correctly understand and handle the Bible passage. But also...

• encourage and train the people in your group to do this for themselves. Don't fall into the trap of spoon-feeding people by simply passing on the information in the Leader's Guide. Then...

• make sure that no Bible study is finished without everyone knowing how the passage is relevant for them. What changes do you all need to make in the light of the things you have been learning? And finally...

• encourage the group to turn all that has been learned and discussed into prayer.

Your Bible-study group is unique, and you are likely to know better than anyone the capabilities, backgrounds and circumstances of the people you are leading. That's why we've designed these guides with a number of optional features. If they're a quiet bunch, you might want to spend longer on *talkabout*. If your time is limited, you can choose to skip *explore more*, or get people to look at these questions at home. Can't get enough of Bible study? Well, some studies have optional extra homework projects. As leader, you can adapt and select the material to the needs of your particular group.

So what's in the Leader's Guide? The main thing that this Leader's Guide will help you to do is to understand the major teaching points in the passage you are studying, and how to apply them. As well as guidance for the questions, the Leader's Guide for each session contains the following important sections:

THE BIG IDEA

One or two key sentences will give you the main point of the session. This is what you should be aiming to have fixed in people's minds as they leave the Bible study. And it's the point you need to head back toward when the discussion goes off at a tangent.

SUMMARY

An overview of the passage, including plenty of useful historical background information.

OPTIONAL EXTRA

Usually this is an introductory activity that ties in with the main theme of the Bible study, and is designed to "break the ice" at the beginning of a session. Or it may be a "homework project" that people can tackle during the week.

So let's take a look at the various different features of a Good Book Guide:

⊕ talkabout

Each session kicks off with a discussion question, based on the group's opinions or experiences. It's designed to get people talking and thinking in a general way about the main subject of the Bible study.

⊡ investigate

The first thing you and your group need to know is what the Bible passage is about, which is the purpose of these questions. But watch out—people may come up with answers based on their experiences or teaching they have heard in the past, without referring to the passage at all. It's amazing how often we can get through a Bible study without actually looking at the Bible! If you're stuck for an answer, the Leader's Guide contains guidance for questions. These are the answers to direct your group to. This information isn't meant to be read out to people—ideally, you want them to discover these answers from the Bible for themselves. Sometimes there are optional follow-up questions (see ⊗ in guidance for questions) to help you help your group get to the answer.

⊡ explore more

These questions generally point people to other relevant parts of the Bible. They are useful for helping your group to see how the passage fits into the "big picture" of the whole Bible. These sections are OPTIONAL—only use them if you have time. Remember that it's better to finish in good time having really grasped one big thing from the passage, than to try and cram everything in.

⊟ apply

We want to encourage you to spend more time working at application—too often, it is simply tacked on at the end. In the Good Book Guides, apply sections are mixed in with the investigate sections of the study. We hope that people will realize that application is not just an optional extra, but rather, the whole purpose of studying the

Bible. We do Bible study so that our lives can be changed by what we hear from God's word. If you skip the application, the Bible study hasn't achieved its purpose.

These questions draw out practical lessons that we can all learn from the Bible passage. You can review what has been learned so far, and think about practical differences that this should make in our churches and our lives. The group gets the opportunity to talk about what they personally have learned.

⊡ getting personal

These can be done at home, but it is well worth allowing a few moments of quiet reflection during the study for each person to think and pray about specific changes they need to make in their own lives. Why not have a time for reporting back at the beginning of the following session, so that everyone can be encouraged and challenged by one another to make application a priority?

↑ pray

In Acts 4:25-30 the first Christians quoted Psalm 2 as they prayed in response to the persecution of the apostles by the Jewish religious leaders. Today however, it's not as common for Christians to base prayers on the truths of God's word as it once was. As a result, our prayers tend to be weak, superficial and self-centered rather than bold, visionary and God-centered.

The prayer section is based on what has been learned from the Bible passage. How different our prayer times would be if we were genuinely responding to what God has said to us through his word.

1

Proverbs 1:1-7
THE BEGINNING OF WISDOM

THE BIG IDEA

Proverbs calls believers to wisdom that transforms all the concrete experiences of life. To find wisdom we must begin with the fear of the Lord: reverencing him for who he is, according to his word.

SUMMARY

Proverbs 1:1-7 is known as the prologue to the book of Proverbs.

Sometimes called the "title," verse 1 introduces not just the prologue but the book: "The proverbs of Solomon, son of David, king of Israel." Those words tell us the first important thing to know: Proverbs' wisdom comes in the context of God's word and God's people.

Verses 2-4 work as a unit with the steadily repeated pattern of infinitives ("to know" and "to understand," "to receive," and "to give"). These verses summarize the book's aim, which is to point the reader toward wisdom in all its various aspects: intellectual in verse 2 (knowing and understanding); ethical in verse 3 (wise dealing, righteousness, justice, equity); and practical in verse 4 (prudence, knowledge, discretion). These multiple categories tell us that when we aim for wisdom, we aim for much more than merely an intellectual process.

Verses 5-6 drive home that aim with a call to pursue wisdom and find its rewards. First, we are called to hear (v 5). Proverbs will keep on driving home the point that hearing—listening humbly to wisdom's words—is the necessary means of seeking and finding wisdom. The rewards are of course multi-faceted, including not only an "increase in learning" but also more practical "guidance," for one who hears and understands these proverbs.

The audience to which this call to wisdom is addressed expands clearly and steadily through these lines. In verse 4, the receivers are "the simple" and "the youth"—which helps confirm the generally accepted understanding that this book was originally used for Israel's leaders-in-training. The call broadens, however, to include "the wise" and "the one who understands" (v 5), communicating the ongoing need to seek and apply wisdom—and the need for humility in the process in order to keep on listening.

From verse 7, the climax of the prologue, we can make two observations which will be crucial to understanding the rest of the book. First, Proverbs' wisdom is found in relationship with the Lord. We are called to fear him, reverencing him for who he is, according to his word. Second, Proverbs' wisdom is the alternative to folly. These two paths of wisdom and folly cut their way through all the wisdom literature, showing the two ways to live and the two destinations toward which they head. This study works through the prologue before taking us to 1 Corinthians 1:18-25 to consider how wisdom is fulfilled in Christ.

OPTIONAL EXTRA

Here's a wisdom-themed twist on a familiar pen-and-paper game. Make up some headlines for a series of lifestyle-advice articles, based on the kinds of subjects that people associate with Proverbs (e.g. work, money, parenting, beauty, marriage, words, etc.). E.g. "Six tips for raising happier kids"; "Seven secrets to getting ahead at work"; "Nine ways to make your money go further." Write each one across the top of a piece of blank paper and the appropriate numbers down the side. Each member writes a "tip" at the bottom of the page, then folds it so it can't be seen, before passing it on to the next person in the circle. At the end of the exercise, unfold the paper and read your "wisdom articles" aloud— probably with humorous (and perhaps contradictory) results. This is intended as a fun way to break the ice at the start of the study, but it also makes the point that we tend to think of Proverbs as a similarly random collection of "tips." But, as we'll see over the next eight studies, this book is far from that; it is a carefully-crafted, life-giving piece of wisdom literature.

GUIDANCE FOR QUESTIONS

1. In our culture, what different "voices" offer wisdom on how to live well?
• How do you decide who to listen to?
This opening question is intended to get your group talking around the theme of wisdom. Cultures throughout history have given ear to various sorts of sages who passed on their wisdom through words; today, we have popular bloggers, personal life coaches, and authors of best-sellers about success, health, and happiness. Many people look for wisdom to well-known media figures like the American Oprah Winfrey, whose self-empowering sayings have been collected and recorded on dozens of website pages— Oprah's proverbs, you might say!

2. Who is the book of Proverbs attributed to? What made his wisdom

different from that of the nations around him? (See 1 Kings 4:29.) Proverbs is attributed to "Solomon, son of David, king of Israel" (1:1). We should note that the content of Proverbs was not all written by Solomon; certain sections of the book are attributed to other wise men. But the great majority of the sayings are indeed attributed to him.

Scripture itself highlights and explains Solomon's distinctive wisdom: "God gave Solomon wisdom and understanding beyond measure, and breadth of mind like the sand on the seashore" (1 Kings 4:29). God had spoken to King Solomon in a dream and invited him to make a request of God. Solomon humbly asked for wisdom—for "an understanding mind to govern your people, that I may discern between good and evil" (1 Kings 3:9). His request was granted: "Behold, I give you a wise and discerning mind, so that none like you has been before you and none like you shall arise after you" (1 Kings 3:12). Solomon's wisdom, then, was insight like that of the peoples around, but it was different: it was God-given insight into how to live in God's world.

• What does verse 1 tell us about where Proverbs fits into the bigger story of God's people in the Old Testament?
Proverbs' wisdom comes in the context of God's word and God's people. Draw your group's attention to the three proper names in verse 1 (Solomon, David, and Israel), which, in one quick sweep, light up the entire Old Testament history of God calling out a people for himself. Solomon was not just a wise king who wrote many of these proverbs. He came from the line of David, of the tribe of Judah: one tribe of the Israelite people, who grew from Abraham into a great nation, according to the Lord's promises.

It's important to fit every Bible book into

the Bible's overarching narrative—its big story of God redeeming a people, through his Son. The historical books unfold the story largely in narrative. The prophetic books let us hear God's voice speaking into the story through his prophets. The psalmists cry out from the midst of the story. The wisdom writers act like commentators who have stepped aside for a few moments to make observations about the story.

EXPLORE MORE
[On Deuteronomy 4:5-8]

• **What does Moses say the people need to do in order to be wise?** They need to "keep" and "do" what the Lord has commanded them.

• **Why did God intend for the Israelites to be wiser than the nations around them?** The Israelites were called to show wisdom to the world, as a testament to God's wise and righteous character.

• **Think forward in Bible history through the Old Testament. Did Israel ultimately succeed or fail in this task, do you think?** As we follow the trajectory of God's people all the way through the story of the Old Testament, they repeatedly fail to fear the Lord and follow his laws. The Israelites did not show wisdom to the world as they were called to do.

• **Think forward in Bible history to the New Testament. How did Jesus fulfill what Israel failed to do?** The fulfillment of God's promises to them arrived in the deliverer who came in David's line—the Lord Jesus, in whom are hidden all the treasures of wisdom and knowledge (Colossians 2:3), and the One whom the apostle Paul calls "the wisdom of God" (1 Corinthians 1:24). (We will return to this passage in question 10 below.) Jesus

came to teach and show us wisdom in the fullest way.

3. Verses 2-4 lay out the book's aim. What will Proverbs equip the hearer to do?

• **Verse 2:** Know and understand wisdom, instruction, and words of insight. These are broadly intellectual.

• **Verse 3:** Deal wisely, with righteousness, justice, and equity. These are broadly ethical.

• **Verse 4:** Act with prudence, knowledge, and discretion. These are broadly practical.

4. What do these different ideas tell you about the nature of wisdom? When we aim for wisdom, we aim for much more than an intellectual process. For example, there is "instruction" in verse 2 and in verse 3—for both the knowing and the doing. Godly wisdom infuses a whole person and all of that person's character and life. If we're looking for a nice neat definition of what wisdom is, it's not here; the prologue gives us a winding mix of weighty wisdom words that the whole book will unpack. We find from the start that this book resists neat ordering and packaging. As a kaleidoscope enables us to glimpse the changing patterns of shapes and colors, so in Proverbs we glimpse the multi-faceted nature of wisdom lived in the flow of daily life. The point is that wisdom touches all of life, as its moments flow not in neatly organized categories but in the ever-changing complexity of human experience.

5. What do verses 5-6...
• **call us to do?**
• **promise as a reward?**
If verses 2-4 summarize the book's aim in regard to wisdom, then verses 5-6 drive

home that aim with a call to pursue wisdom and find its rewards. The first and crucial part of the call is indeed to hear (v 5). Proverbs will keep on driving home the point that hearing—listening humbly to wisdom's words—is the necessary means of seeking and finding wisdom. The rewards are of course multi-faceted, including not only an "increase in learning" but also more practical "guidance," for one who hears and understands these proverbs.

6. Who is the book's wisdom addressed to (v 4, 5)? In verse 4, the receivers are "the simple" and "the youth." It is generally accepted that this book was originally used for Israel's leaders-in-training. The word "simple" probably means naïve or untaught, as are many young people; these words work together. In verse 5 the call extends to "the wise" and to "the one who understands," communicating the ongoing need to seek and apply wisdom—and the need for humility in the process in order to keep on listening. This is a book not just for youth; this wisdom is continually needed by all of us: young and old, male and female.

7. APPLY: Proverbs warns against ever thinking we've outgrown the need to seek wisdom. How can we tell if we're in danger of having that attitude? Allow your group to share ideas and examples from their own lives. This attitude may exhibit itself in prayerlessness, a reluctance to seek counsel from others, or a resistance to correction.

• **What does it look like to continue to stop, listen, and learn as we grow in Christian maturity?** You might want to talk about some godly older saints in your church who exemplify this sort of humble, teachable attitude.

8. What "opposites" does [Proverbs 1:7] set up? These two parallel lines of poetry set up a contrast between wisdom and folly. This verse makes it clear: there is the way of wisdom, which begins with the fear of the Lord, and there is the way of folly, in which wisdom is despised and rejected. These two lines actually set up an interesting antithetic parallelism (two paired lines that say quite opposite things). You might expect that the "fools" in line 2 would contrast directly with the *wise* in line 1. But there are no wise people in line 1. It is the Lord himself, and the fear of him, that these fools are set against. The fools reject that relationship; ultimately it is the Lord himself they despise. It's a helpful truth to remember: people choosing the path of folly don't need just an argument; they need to meet a person.

9. What does it mean to fear the Lord, do you think? This will be a key phrase throughout the book, so push your group to something specific here. Fearing the Lord means reverencing him for who he is, according to his word. This is the relationship that determines everything—fearing him leads to listening, following, and repenting. Fearing him is the starting point for all these weighty wisdom words of verses 2-6. It's the thing that gets the kaleidoscope turning. How gracious of God to reveal himself to us and to redeem us, so that we are able to fear him as his beloved people.

⌄

• **Why is it significant that verse 7 says "The fear of the LORD [Yahweh]", not "the fear of God"?** *Yahweh* is a special name for God; it is the name God gave Moses to use in telling the people of Israel who it was that sent him to rescue them from Egypt (Exodus 3:15). The LORD is the One who mercifully rescues a sinful people according to his promises, finally through his Son. Proverbs is not merely a collection of sayings but rather a book about relationship with God.

10. Read 1 Corinthians 1:18-25. How does Jesus, "the wisdom of God" (v 24), bring about our salvation? What else strikes you from these verses? It is through "the word of the cross" (v 18)— the cross where Jesus took on our sin and suffered God's wrath in our place. This inversion of weakness and strength looks foolish in the world's eyes, but those of us who have had our eyes opened by the Spirit can see Christ and the message of his crucifixion for what they are: "The power of God and the wisdom of God" (v 24).

11. APPLY: In what areas of your life do you most feel in need of wisdom? What would it look like to fear the Lord in these circumstances? Encourage your group to share openly, but appropriately, about the circumstances they're struggling to navigate wisely. Fearing the Lord in these circumstances likely includes coming to his word humbly and in prayer; seeking to obey his commands and honor his priorities as they are laid out in his word; and not railing against him but submitting to his sovereignty.

12. APPLY: "People choosing the path of folly don't need just an argument; they need to meet a person." How have you seen that to be true in your own experience? Your group likely have examples of non-Christian friends or family who have heard the arguments but are yet to see who Jesus really is. The cross is "folly" to them (1 Corinthians 1:18).

• How should that shape the way you

seek to speak wisdom into the lives of others (both Christians and non-Christians)? We should always take people back to Jesus. Our evangelism will always be deficient if we only ever present the evidence for the resurrection, or the historicity of the Gospels. These things are helpful, but on their own they won't draw people away from the path of folly. Only encountering Jesus—through his word, in the power of his Spirit—will. When counselling Christians against foolish choices or sinful behavior, we likewise need to take them to Christ—reminding them of what he's done, setting forth the cross, and appealing to them to live in the light of that, rather than only laying down a list of dos and don'ts.

2 Proverbs 1:8 – 7:27
TWO PATHS

THE BIG IDEA

The Lord calls us to follow the path of wisdom and avoid the path of folly—and he lovingly instructs us how to do this through his word.

SUMMARY

We've heard the prologue calling us to wisdom and its fruit—and now Proverbs begins to develop that call. After the prologue, chapters 1 – 9 make up the first main section of the book. This wisdom teaching can be organized in various ways, but many agree there are ten main instructions that begin with "My son." The instructions are interspersed with several "wisdom sections": an address by Wisdom (personified) (as in 1:20-33) or a poem about wisdom (as we will see in chapter 3), or another kind of passage on wisdom. All of this can be outlined as follows:

- Instruction 1 (1:8-19)
  - Wisdom section 1 (1:20-33)
- Instruction 2 (2:1-22)
- Instruction 3 (3:1-12)
  - Wisdom section 2 (3:13-20)
- Instruction 4 (3:21-35)
- Instruction 5 (4:1-9)
- Instruction 6 (4:10-19)
- Instruction 7 (4:20-27)
- Instruction 8 (5:1-23)
  - Wisdom section 3 (6:1-19)
- Instruction 9 (6:20-35)
- Instruction 10 (7:1-27)
  - Wisdom section 4 (8:1-36)
  - Wisdom section 5 (9:1-18)

The first part of this study will take us through the rest of Proverbs 1, with a fatherly instruction and a personal address from Wisdom personified as a woman.

The setting of 1:8-19 is a warm, live one in which father and mother together are pictured as offering their son "instruction" and "teaching". The structure of this teaching looks like this:

- Opening call to hear (v 8-9)
- Main instruction (v 10)
- Temptation not to hear (v 11-14)
- Reasons to hear (v 15-18)
- Concluding lesson (v 19)

The wisdom section in 1:20-33 pictures wisdom as a woman named Wisdom. This is an example of personification: a figure of speech in which something nonhuman is pictured as though it were a person. We know we're just pretending with these pictures, but the pictures let us imagine in a way that shows us truth.

After Wisdom is introduced (v 20-21), she speaks (v 22-33). Her predominantly negative warning is laced with a quick flash of positive promise, as a brief outline suggests:

- Opening reproach (v 22)
- Promise for those who will hear (v 23)
- Warning for those who refuse to hear (v 24-31)
- Summary teaching: two ways and two ends (v 32-33)

The second part of the study provides readers with a three-question framework with which to study any of the remaining instructions.

OPTIONAL EXTRA

Print or write out a variety of proverbs (some biblical, some not) on slips of paper.

Can your group successfully identify which is which? Make the point that when we think of Proverbs, what often comes first to mind is the collection of short sayings that begin in chapter 10. But before we dive too quickly into those proverbs, we need to begin in the way this book leads us to begin: with the foundation of wisdom, based on fearing the Lord.

GUIDANCE FOR QUESTIONS

1. What is some of the best advice you received as a child, from parents or teachers? The idea of this question is to set the tone for the instructions in Proverbs 1 – 9, which each begin "My son." The image is of a warm family setting, with father and mother lovingly urging a young man to listen to their wisdom. If some members of your group had more complicated upbringings, encourage them to think about the advice they've received from parental figures.

2. What is the son called to do, and what is the reward for doing that (v 8-9)? The opening call to hear (v 8a) is key. It continues the prologue's ringing call (v 5a), and each instruction in the following chapters will open with some version of it. Proverbs does not say, *Here, affirm this list of truths.* It says, *Hear these words that are coming to you live!* Verse 9 holds out just for a moment an enticing picture of how blessed this son's life will be if he listens. The graceful garland and pendants bring to our imaginations concrete images of beauty and riches, along with connotations of success and favor. Although the instruction in Proverbs might seem hard, the rewards are as wonderful as the most beautiful adornments and gems we can imagine.

• **What is the alternative to hearing (suggested in v 8b)?** The son's two possible responses are anticipated in the

parallel commands: the positive command to "hear" and the negative command to "forsake not." True hearing in fact would mean not forsaking. In Proverbs true hearing, like true knowing, is more than something that happens in a person's head. It always involves life-altering results, as words penetrate the heart and then transform actions.

3. What instruction does the father give to his son? ("Do not..." v 10, 15) The kernel of the instruction comes in verse 10: "If sinners entice you, do not consent." In verses 11-14, the father gives a sample of the sinners' enticing voices, which try to persuade the son to hear and follow them. In verse 15 the father pictures a "way" or "path" on which the son must not walk, along with such companions.

• **And why? ("For..." v 16-19)** The sinners' path is a way of "evil," along which these men are not just walking but running (v 16). Birds are aware enough not to fly into a net that they see someone spreading in front of them; these men, by ironic contrast, are so foolish that they are in effect setting an ambush for themselves (v 17, 18a). In later sections Proverbs will make vivid the ways in which cruelty and violence destroy the lives not just of others but finally of the perpetrators themselves. The instruction's conclusion (v 19) draws out this image into a larger lesson. The path of sin leads to destruction; it is a direction of heart and action that takes away life. In the second half of this study it will be important that your group have grasped this image of "two paths"— wisdom and folly—so be sure to draw your group's attention to it here.

4. APPLY: At its most basic level, this instruction warns youths against

joining gangs of looters! What other, broader applications does this passage suggest to us? This passage warns us all against the enticement of seeking reward along the wrong path, and against listening to the wrong voice. Like the son, we too will be thrust into scenarios where words are being offered, in the context of various relationships—some helpful, some dangerous. The question is: Whose words will we hear?

5. What is Wisdom doing, and where (v 20-21)? Wisdom gives a warning and promise similar to the father's in verses 8-19, but in contrast to the intimate family scene, Wisdom calls out in the most public context. Four parallel verbs emphasize that her words are for all to hear: "cries aloud," "raises her voice" (1:20), "cries out," and "speaks" (v 21). And four settings light up the parts of a city where all sorts of people would gather for the main activities of life: "the street," where they live and "the markets," where they buy and sell (v 20); "the head of the noisy streets," where everybody can see and hear and "the entrance of the city gates," where civic leaders would make decisions (v 21). This is a powerful picture of the way God so fully reveals himself through his word.

- **Who is she speaking to, and what does she long for them to do (v 22-23)?** Verse 22 addresses three categories of people along the path of foolishness: the "simple" (the naïve or immature that we saw in the prologue); the "scoffers" (fools that stand out, delighting in their scoffing); and "fools" in general, who (as in v 7) "hate knowledge." Wisdom doesn't start out by simply condemning them; she mixes condemnation with a yearning for their foolishness to end, repeating those words "How long?" in a way that

is reminiscent of God's words calling to Israel through his prophets (e.g. Jeremiah 4:14; Hosea 8:5). Wisdom's next words offer a promise that rings out even more strikingly: if these people will "turn" to her when she rebukes them, then, she says, "I will pour out my spirit to you; I will make my words known to you" (Proverbs 1:23).

NOTE: Some in your group may ask about the significance of the fact that wisdom is personified as a woman, not a man. Part of the reason may be that, as with French and Spanish, Hebrew is a language with masculine and feminine nouns. So, according to the commentator Bruce Waltke, "The abstract noun *hokmâ* ["wisdom" in Hebrew] is feminine and accordingly becomes personified as a woman" (*The Book of Proverbs Chapters 1-15*, p 83). The Hebrew noun for "folly" is also feminine, and we shall meet the woman named Folly later on, in chapter 9. Proverbs is not telling us that wisdom itself is female; no, Proverbs is picturing or personifying wisdom as a woman. The best way to understand this Wisdom is to look at the picture closely. What is this woman like? What is she doing? What does this tell us about wisdom?

6. What do the following verses tell us about the possible responses to Wisdom, and the consequences of them? Try to help your group get into the structure of the passage by pointing them to linking words, e.g. "If you … I will"; "Because … I will"; "Because … Therefore."

- **Verses 24-28:** Wisdom has called and has stretched out her hand, and people have refused to listen (v 24; see v 25); therefore ("therefore" is implied at the start of v 26) when calamity and terror come on them and they call to her, she will not answer (v 26-28). In fact, she will laugh at their distress (see link with Psalm 2:4 in Explore More).

• **Verses 29-31:** This second section repeats much of the previous one but focuses more on the foolish ones themselves— and, significantly, adds that they "did not choose the fear of the LORD" (v 29b). Interestingly, verse 30 goes on to repeat verse 25 almost exactly, yet in light of verse 29 we understand that rejecting Wisdom's counsel and reproof means rejecting the fear of the Lord.

• **Verses 32-33:** These final verses clarify the message: Wisdom's words are the key. Turn away from her call and be destroyed (v 32), or "listen to me" and dwell secure (v 33).

7. Look again at this picture of Wisdom. What does she show us about God?

Wisdom's voice helps us grasp how God, through his word, mercifully speaks into every part of our lives as human beings. She helps us understand God's love and desire for us to turn to him, and his grace in pouring out his Spirit on us when we repent and believe his word. Wisdom's voice warns us of God's condemnation of sin and the coming judgment, when it will be too late to repent. And she reminds us that hearing and following God's word is not a matter of being happier but a matter of life and death: eternal security vs. eternal destruction.

EXPLORE MORE

Look up some of the following passages and compare them to Proverbs 1:20-33. How does Wisdom echo God's word in these other parts of Scripture?

• **Jeremiah 4:14 and Numbers 14:11, 27.** Help your group see the link between God's words calling to Israel through Jeremiah, and Wisdom's words in Proverbs 2:22.

• **Joel 2:28-29 and Acts 2:17.** There's a clear resonance between Proverbs 1:23 and the similarly worded promise in Joel 2:28-9 (see also Isaiah 32:15). The New Testament picks up these promises—most notably in Acts 2:17, as the apostle Peter quotes the prophet Joel to explain the outpouring of the Holy Spirit at Pentecost.

• **Psalm 2:4.** This picture of God in the heavens laughing—holding in derision those earthly kings who set themselves against him—finds an echo in Proverbs 1:26.

Choose two of the remaining nine instruction sections, and use questions 7 and 8 to guide you through them. If your group is relatively confident in handling the Bible, you could split them into pairs and get each pair to look at two different instructions, before reporting back to the group as a whole. Alternatively, you could work through Instructions 2 and 3 all together, and suggest that group members use the same framework to study Instructions 4 – 10 at home before the next session. The answers below are given for Instruction 2 (2:1-22) and Instruction 3 (3:1-12). For guidance on Proverbs 3:21 – 7:27, see *Proverbs For You* by Kathleen Nielson, chapters 2 – 4.

8. *First instruction of your choice:* What is the structure of this "instruction"?

• IF (2:1-4): Three "ifs" set up a condition for the whole rest of the poem. The father is saying, *If you open your heart wide to wisdom…*

• THEN/FOR (v 5-8): The "then" is a result that will occur *if* the condition is met. Verse 5 is amazing—we can understand the fear of the Lord! Why? "For the LORD gives wisdom" (v 6).

- THEN/FOR (v 9-15): Verses 9-15 describe the process of wisdom coming into our heart and soul, transforming our understanding and our actions. We will then be guarded by discretion and delivered from those given to evil, who are walking not on wisdom's paths but on crooked ones.
- SO/FOR (v 16-19): These "so's" are conclusions. Here the conclusion is deliverance from "the forbidden woman," a figure we will meet again.
- SO/FOR (v 20-22): The final "so" pictures the son walking in "the way of the good" and "the paths of the righteous" (v 20). The concluding "for" (v 21-22) summarizes the two ways: that of the upright, who will inhabit and remain in the land, and that of the wicked, who will be cut off from the land.

- **What is the key idea of this instruction?** The key idea is that the Lord gives treasures of wisdom through his word, if we open our hearts to receive it. This is an overwhelmingly encouraging instruction. Again we are reminded that all these treasures flow from a relationship with him, in which we reverence him for who he is according to his word—and then as we walk forward in the security of that relationship.

- **How are the two paths—wisdom and folly—made vivid in this passage?** The path of wisdom is described as protected, pleasant, and leading to a place of permanent security—contrasting with the crooked path, where evil men and women are sinking down to death. Listening, we see and recoil from that deadly path and are drawn toward the path of life. In short, if the message of the first instruction (1:8-19) was to stay off the bad

guys' path, the message of this one is to seek the good path.

9. Second instruction of your choice: What is the structure of this "instruction"? In 3:1-12 six commands flesh out what it means to fear the Lord. Each command is linked to a motivation or reward for obeying that command. Notice how the progression of commands focuses in the very center on the fear of the Lord (3:7b), and moves in the end toward the reward of a relationship with the Lord himself as our loving father, who disciplines us because he delights in us (v 12).

- **What is the key idea of this instruction?** Fearing the Lord involves a life of obeying his word—and it brings a life overflowing with his love and blessing.

- **How are the two paths—wisdom and folly—made vivid in this passage?** This instruction peers almost completely down the good path, with only hints of the path of folly, which would involve turning away from the word of the Lord. Blessings overflow along the path of learning to trust and obey the word of the Lord—that is, walking in fear of him. In short, if the message of the first instruction was to stay off the bad guys' path (1:8-19), and the message of the second was to seek the good path (2:1-22), then the message of this third instruction is to walk this path obediently—and find the Lord's presence and blessing along the way.

EXPLORE MORE
[Read Proverbs 3:13-20] What are wisdom's value (v 14-15) and benefits (v 16-18)? Her value is immeasurable; it can be expressed only through imagery, by comparison with the most valuable earthly treasures: silver, gold, and jewels (v 14-15;

recall 2:4). These are all most highly valued, but "nothing you desire can compare with her." Her benefits include riches and honor, but first, in her right hand, long life—life described in 3:17 as ways of pleasantness and paths of peace.

What other parts of the Bible are you reminded of as you read this poem? How does it turn your thoughts to the Lord Jesus? The image of the tree of life in verse 18 pulls our thoughts ahead to eternal life, and back to the Garden of Eden, where Adam and Eve were cut off from the tree of life for their sin (Genesis 3:24). In verses 19-20 our thoughts turn to Jesus, through whom and for whom all things were created (Colossians 1:16). He is the merciful Savior, who came close and made it possible for us to be reconciled with our Creator, through his death on our behalf and his resurrection from the dead.

10. APPLY: Has there been a time when God's word called you from the path of folly, or a time when you were able to give a call to someone heading down that path?

11. APPLY: In what ways have you have experienced the blessings of walking the path of wisdom, fearing the Lord? These questions aim to help your group think how they've seen the "two paths" of wisdom and folly vividly in their own lives, as they have listened to God's word and trusted the Lord Jesus revealed in that word. Hopefully your group will be eager to share stories of God's mercy and goodness to them in the past, but make sure you have a few of your own ready in case you need to get the ball rolling.

NOTE: The next study will pick up in Proverbs 8. Depending on how much of chapters 2 – 7 you were able to cover in this study, you may want to encourage your group to read these passages at home before the next study. You could suggest that they use the three-step framework outlined in questions 8 and 9 to help them.

3 Proverbs 8:1 – 9:18
WOMEN CALLING

BIG IDEA
The way of wisdom is precious, beautiful and life-giving—and is ours in Christ Jesus. The way of folly offers only a cheap imitation—and ultimately leads to death.

SUMMARY
Chapters 8 and 9 contain the fourth and fifth wisdom sections of this first part of Proverbs (chapters 1 – 9).

After the previous instructions, the wisdom section in chapter 8 feels climactic. As in 1:20-33, here we find Wisdom again calling and raising her voice in public places, where people of all kinds are likely and able to hear. The speech in chapter 8 falls into three main sections between the introduction (v 1-3) and the concluding call (v 32-36). First, Wisdom speaks about the nature of her words (v 4-11). Second, she speaks of the benefits she brings (v 12-21). Third, she speaks of her identity (v 22-31). In these sections, Wisdom is revealing herself more and more clearly; it's as if she is lifting her veil, and we can only marvel at what we get to see.

If chapter 8 is the high point of the book's first section, chapter 9 is the perfect landing point, and the perfect preparation for the next section to come. With all these voices calling, it's clear that we must respond. That's what the final chapter of this section asks us to do.

In Proverbs 9, a beginning section and an end section are balanced against each other. More specifically, two women are directly competing against each other: Wisdom (9:1-6) and Folly (v 13-18). Most agree that these are both personifications, picturing for us what wisdom and folly are all about. What stands out is that Folly offers the opposite of what Wisdom offers: ultimately, death vs. life.

These two directly contrasting figures are placed at either end of the chapter—with wise instruction in between (v 7-12). That middle section connects thematically in both directions, to Wisdom and to Folly. But right in its center comes the main point of the chapter—and, indeed, a reprise of the main point of the whole book: "The fear of the LORD is the beginning of wisdom, and the knowledge of the Holy One is insight" (v 10).

OPTIONAL EXTRA

How good are your group at identifying the voices calling out to them? Blindfold one group member and invite other people to read out a proverb while disguising their voice. Can the blindfolded person identify who is calling?

If you encouraged your group to study Proverbs 2 – 7 at home between the last study and this one, allow time for people to share what struck, challenged, or excited them, before moving on to chapter 8.

GUIDANCE FOR QUESTIONS

1. Have you ever been duped into buying a cheap imitation of the real deal? How did it work out, and how did you feel? This question is intended to get people talking at the start of the study. Explain that later in today's passage we'll see Wisdom and Folly making similar-sounding offers to the simple—but they are radically different, and each one leads to very different consequences.

2. What do we learn about Wisdom's…

• **words? (v 4-11)** Her words are for everyone (v 4), although with a familiar focus on the simple (v 5). They can be trusted for she will speak "noble things" and "what is right," and "utter truth" and words that are "righteous" and "straight" (v 6-9). Wisdom's worth is better than silver or gold (v 10-11). We could summarize these verses like this: *Listen! My words will tell you truth—truth more valuable than anything else you could ever seek.*

• **benefits? (v 12-21)** As in the book's prologue, we are promised "prudence," "knowledge," "discretion," "wisdom," and "insight" (v 12-14). And again the stated foundation is "the fear of the LORD" (v 13a). Verses 15-16 apply her benefits specifically to political leaders, emphasizing the just rule that Wisdom enables kings, rulers, princes, and nobles to exercise. Verses 18-21 overflow with the treasures of the love promised in verse 17: riches and honor, wealth and righteousness. This is an "inheritance" that outlasts death (v 21); our gaze is directed toward eternal treasure for those who seek after wisdom with all their hearts.

3. What is the overall mood of verses 22-31? We mustn't miss the overflowing joy and delight of this passage. Notice how the delight lands on the same audience that Wisdom addresses: the "children of man" (v 4b; v 31b). Wisdom's call in Proverbs is not an abstract call to virtue; it is the Lord's call to the human beings he created in his image, for his glory—and joy!

• **How do these words point us forward to what the New Testament reveals about Christ? (See John 1:1-3, Colossians 1:15-17 and 2:3)** Wisdom is presenting herself as God's agent of creation: the one through whom all things were made. As such, she is claiming the role that the New Testament attributes to God's Son. So, in light of all of Scripture, we can say that this picture in Proverbs, while not being Christ, points ahead toward Christ. From our vantage point in salvation's story, we get to hear the New Testament writers fully celebrating the Word (John 1:1-3), Jesus Christ, "in whom are hidden all the treasures of wisdom and knowledge" (Colossians 2:3).

4. How do the concluding verses (v 32-36) remind us of the two paths pictured throughout Proverbs? The invitation is to "hear instruction and be wise," and the promise is blessing (v 33, 34; see also 3:13) for those who will watch at Wisdom's gates and wait beside her doors. The final two verses give concluding clarity to the two paths: "Whoever finds me finds life," says Wisdom; "all who hate me love death" (v 35-36).

5. APPLY: Do you tend to associate wisdom (living God's way) with the kind of joy and delight we see in chapter 8 or with something more dour? Why might that be, do you think? How can

we keep the breathtaking goodness of God's wisdom in view? Encourage your group to share ideas. Often we obey out of a sense of duty, or we do things because "that's what Christians do"—while suspecting that we'd be having more fun if we weren't believers. Or we put up with God's restrictions now because we want to enjoy heaven later. Or it may be that we have in mind passages such as Luke 9:23-25, where Jesus speaks about taking up one's cross to follow him. To live wisely we need to have a realistic view of the cost, but also a brighter view of the blessings flowing from the God who created all things good. Chapter 8's poetry shows us that wisdom is what is truly beautiful, precious, good, and life-giving—and so a life lived wisely, in fear of the Lord, will be all those things too.

6. Compare the woman Wisdom (9:1-6) with the woman Folly (v 7-12).

• **What similarities do you see?** Both women are at their house; both women call to "whoever is simple" and the one who "lacks sense"; both women promise satisfying food and drink.

• **What are the differences?** Wisdom has done the work, from down-and-dirty to perfect finishing touches: from hewing out great pillars to slaughtering beasts for meat, to mixing the wine, to setting the table. She has done it all for her guests; all they have to do is come in and feast with her. In contrast to Wisdom, who works so hard, Folly is sitting down by her door. She offers not wine that she has mixed herself but stolen water (v 17). Folly has no creativity by which to make anything herself; she can only imitate. The most important difference is where Wisdom and Folly lead: one to life (v 6) and the other to death (v 18).

EXPLORE MORE

The theme of feasting in the presence of the Lord is one which resonates throughout Scripture. Read one or more of the following passages [Exodus 24:9-11; Isaiah 25:6; John 6:35, 50-51; Revelation 19:6-9]. How do they echo the themes we see in Proverbs 9:1-6? The idea of this Explore More is to stand back and enjoy how this theme connects and grows throughout the Scriptures. In Exodus 24, Moses and seventy of the elders go up on the mountain and glimpse the shining glory of God's presence. Moses sums up what they did there: "They beheld God, and ate and drank" (Exodus 24:11). Later, the prophets spoke of future feasting in God's presence. Isaiah, for example, pictures a scene that resonates closely with Wisdom's feast (Isaiah 25:6).

Resonances continue to grow as the redemptive story unfolds. The promised Lamb of God, God's own Son, comes to save his people, and he not only multiplies bread and feeds crowds of thousands, but says, "I am the bread of life" (John 6:35). And he explains what he will do for them so that they can eat and drink and live: he will lay down his life (John 6:50-51). He will do all the work of salvation on their behalf so that they can live. The book of Revelation ties together this theme of feasting with more pictures, again letting us peer into realities that we cannot yet fully understand. As the bride of Christ, we believers look forward to that marriage supper of the Lamb, when we will be clothed in "fine linen, bright and pure" (Revelation 19:6-9), which, we're told, is "the righteous deeds of the saints." We're also told that "it was granted [the bride, i.e. the church] to clothe herself" in this linen. It was granted to us to be righteous because someone else did the work for us, on our behalf. Jesus died in our

place and rose again. Trusting in him, we get to go in to the feast.

Wisdom has done the work, and invites us into her house, to feast on the bread and wine she has prepared for us.

Not until we get to the end of the story ourselves, when Jesus comes again, will we understand exactly how these themes all come together. But the Scriptures are full of hints: hints that feed our souls in the meantime.

7. What, according to verse 10, is the key to choosing Wisdom over Folly? The key is in the chapter's center—it is fearing the Lord. This verse not only holds the chapter together; it also forms an *inclusio* (a kind of sandwich) with the same key statement of the prologue in 1:7; in fact, these two verses hold together the whole first section of the book.

8. What else marks the wise from the foolish (v 7-9)? As we follow the Lord, fearing him, we are enabled to receive wise words wisely. That's what this middle section emphasizes: 9:7-9 contrasts the ways in which a wise and a foolish person receive instruction. In sum, the fool hates and abuses the teacher; the wise man loves the teacher and learns wisdom.

9. Proverbs 9:10 serves as a bookend with the same statement in the prologue (1:7). What have we learned about living in the fear of the Lord since then? This is an opportunity to recap some of the things we've seen over the course of these first three studies in Proverbs 1 – 9. Several times, we've seen that the fear of the Lord is the opposite of folly. It leads to life, whereas folly leads to death. It is, at heart, a reverent relationship with God that begins and grows through listening to his voice (2:5). God calls out to us through his word, longing for us to listen and rightly fear him (1:20-2). To fear the Lord is to hate evil (8:13). It leads to rich blessing as we enjoy a relationship with him (chapter 8). This relationship is only made possible through Christ, our wisdom from God, whose cross looks foolish to the world but is the means of our salvation (1 Corinthians 1:18-25).

10. APPLY: How do you experience the conflicting voices of Wisdom and Folly calling in your everyday life? In what ways do they make similar offers but with very different consequences? Encourage your group to share ideas. For example, Folly calls us to satisfy our appetites—through acquiring material possessions, or bingeing on food or TV, or viewing pornography. Wisdom calls us to find eternal satisfaction in the bread of life, the Lord Jesus; to enjoy good things as good gifts from him; and to reject sinful things as not truly satisfying. Folly calls us to seek security—through amassing more wealth, or earning the respect of others, or pursuing romantic relationships. Wisdom calls us to find security in the Lord, who is sovereign and who keeps his promises, while we hold his gifts lightly.

11. APPLY: How can we get better at being the kind of people who rightly give and receive wise correction? It comes back, of course, to fearing the Lord. If we have a reverent view of God's holiness, we won't be the sort of people who assume we're fine as we are. And if we fear the Lord, we won't fear other people. Their reproof or correction won't crush us, nor will we be distraught at the thought of losing their good opinion. Instead, we'll be keen to grow in godliness, as our blind spots are pointed out to us. In fact, we'll be constantly corrected by God's word. When it comes to giving correction, some of us are quick to speak the truth but with little love (Ephesians 4:15). But in a church context, it's perhaps more likely that we're reticent to speak truth at all, as we don't want to risk our relationships. The suggestion in these verses is that when we encounter abuse and hatred in response to correction, that says more about the hearer than it does about the speaker. If we're never in a position to give and receive this kind of correction, the problem may be that we're not close enough to anyone—wise people let others see behind the "Sunday morning charade"!

Proverbs 10:1-32

INTO THE SWIRL

BIG IDEA

Through poetry, with its parallelism and imagery, Proverbs speaks wisdom into the swirl of everyday life. One theme stands out: wise living means restraining our tongues and using them to bring life to others.

SUMMARY

The book's opening section (chapters 1 – 9) has helped us understand the beginning of wisdom as the fear of the Lord. On that foundation we are prepared to receive the instruction of the "proverbs proper," beginning in chapter 10 with a collection called "The proverbs of Solomon" (10:1 – 22:16). Proverbs 10 immerses us immediately in a variety of themes that swirl all around us. While the same cycling repetition was evident in the first nine chapters, that was like swimming in a bay with lots of strong currents; now in chapter 10 we're out in the open ocean, often feeling tossed around from one theme to another, and back and forth. While our instinct is to want to organize the Proverbs into different themes, God chose to give them to us in this swirl for a reason (as we'll consider in question 6).

The "nutshell" wisdom of these proverbs comes to us in condensed poetry, using both imagery and parallelism to communicate powerfully. The first half of the study helps us to see how the poetry works, by walking us through the parallelism in 10:1-5. The second half of the study takes us through the rest of chapter 10, giving particular attention to the theme of words.

OPTIONAL EXTRA

At the start of your study, provide some hardy candy (boiled sweets) and discuss the relative merits of "crunching" versus "sucking." If you're confident that no dental damage will be done, you could set up a challenge: one group member must eat their candy by crunching and another by sucking. Who finished faster? But who enjoyed the candy more? Make the point that this is a useful image for approaching the proverbs: as with hard candy, if you bite down fast, you just "break your teeth"; but if you suck on a proverb slowly, the flavor unfolds.

GUIDANCE FOR QUESTIONS

1. What are some of your favorite poems or song lyrics? What is it about the words that makes them so

powerful? Part of what makes poetry (and songs) so powerful is the way that they express ideas through imagery and wordplay. The Proverbs are no different. However, while many poems and songs make use of rhythm and rhyme (which cannot easily be translated), the poetry in Proverbs relies more on the "rhyme" of *thoughts* than the rhyme of *sounds*. Fortunately for us, these still "work" when translated into English—it is a marvel that God set up his word to work in this way!

2. What themes from Proverbs 1 – 9 do you see repeated here [in Proverbs 10:1-5]? Proverbs 10:1-5 makes clear the fundamental contrast introduced in chapters 1 – 9: that of wisdom and folly (or righteousness and wickedness). In verse 1 we again meet the young man and his father and mother. 1:8 and 6:20 showed them both teaching him; here we have the father and mother (joined in the couplet) experiencing the joy and the sorrow of sons who follow either wisdom or folly. The "righteous" are the people walking wisdom's path, in the fear of the Lord. This doesn't mean they're perfect. In fact, often the point is that they listen to rebuke, and they repent and change. The "wicked," by contrast, walk folly's path: not listening, and heading toward death rather than life.

3. Look at verses 1, 4, and 5. What opposite ideas are held up as contrasts (antithetic parallelism)? The aim of this question is to encourage your group to look at each proverb slowly and carefully, and to practice thinking in terms of parallelisms. Verse 1: wise son = glad father v foolish son = sad mother. Verse 4: slack hand = poverty v diligent hand = riches. Verse 5: gathering in summer = prudent v sleeping in harvest = shame.

4. If you only had the first line of the following verses in front of you, how might you expect the second line to go?

- **Verse 2:** We might expect something like, *Treasures gained by wickedness do not profit, but treasures gained by righteousness do profit.*

- **Verse 3:** We might expect, *The Lord does not let the righteous go hungry, but he lets the wicked go hungry.*

5. What is surprising about what the second line actually says, and what does that teach us?

- **Verse 2:** The second line does not even mention treasure. Instead all we have in line 2 is righteousness: it is righteousness itself that is the great treasure, and that does not just bring some temporary profit; it actually delivers from death.

- **Verse 3:** We find not just that the Lord lets the wicked go hungry, but that he actively "thwarts" not the hunger but the "craving" of the wicked. This proverb reveals so much: God's care for those who follow him; God's punishment of those rebelling against him; and also the nature of those who rebel.

NOTE: Some in your group may object to verse 4 on the basis that there are many Christians around the world who do go hungry. Proverbs is well known for associating good rewards with good behavior, and bad consequences with bad behavior. (Many refer to this as Proverbs' "character-consequence" connection.) The first thing to say about verse 4 is that it is often true. According to the way the Creator God set up his world, laziness, for example, often does cause poverty, and diligent work usually brings good results (see also v 5). But the second thing to say is that it is not

always true. The proverbs are not rules or promises. They give insight into the order of God's creation, but that order has been disrupted by sin. That's why, along with the many proverbs connecting good rewards with good behavior, come the ones that acknowledge that sometimes it's the other way round. Before 10:4 comes 10:2, where we see that sometimes treasures are gained by wickedness. We need to read all the proverbs.

6. How many different themes or situations does this chapter speak into? List as many as you can. Some themes we encounter include: work (v 5), reputation (v 7), words (v 8 and elsewhere), conflict (v 12), wealth (v 15), and laziness (v 26). The aim of this question is not so much to identify all the different themes but to appreciate how varied they are. It feels more like a playlist on shuffle than a concept album! Such varied themes continue to swirl all around us throughout most of the rest of the book.

- **Why did God give us the Proverbs in such a diverse swirl, rather than grouped by theme, do you think?** Proverbs does reflect the style of wisdom literature found in a number of ancient cultures. As a Bible book, however, Proverbs is breathed out by God the divine author, written and edited by Solomon and a few others, all under God's sovereign hand. And so our question is a good one: why did God give us the proverbs in this swirling form? Perhaps it's because Proverbs' wisdom invades every part of life, and the book actually shows us that real-life process. We human beings don't wake up in the morning and deal first with our marriage and family issues, and then our money issues, and then our tongue, all in a logically planned order. No—from the moment we wake, life comes at us in the same kind of fluid chaos that Proverbs presents, as it teaches us that wisdom is applying God's truth to all of it, all of life, in all its messiness! How wonderful that God sees and speaks into what so often feels like the chaos of our lives. Plus, if the themes were organized into categories, we would probably just pick the categories that we think we need or that we want to focus on. Finally, this amazing swirl of proverbs makes vivid the searching process described in the book's first section: aiming to understand the "riddles" of wise words (1:6) and searching for wisdom as for hidden treasures (2:4).

7. What different things does this chapter say about our words? What images and patterns do you notice?
- **Verse 6**
- **Verse 8**
- **Verse 10**
- **Verse 11**
- **Verse 18**
- **Verse 19**
- **Verse 20**
- **Verse 32**

Again, the aim here is to get your group reading slowly and chewing over the relevant proverbs. Verse 6 continues the contrast between the righteous and the wicked. This wicked person is evidently talking, but his speech is like a deceptive cover. Violent thoughts and intents lurk behind his words. The same picture is repeated in Proverbs 10:11, with a more direct contrast. The wicked hides evil behind his words; by contrast, the righteous sends forth good through his words. Even though the wicked person is three times described as "concealing" evil behind his words (v 6b, 11b, 18a), his words still bubble forth. He's a "babbling fool" (v 8b, 10b).

The prudent person "restrains" his lips, but for the evil person "words are many" and "transgression is not lacking" (v 19). When the wise person *does* speak, what comes out is beautiful (v 20).

8. Where do our words come from, according to these proverbs? What is inside a person is the key. Hidden inside the evil person, behind his babbling words, is violence and evil intent. But inside the righteous person we find something very different (v 8): a heart open to wisdom, to wise words—ultimately to the commandments of God's law. (Note also the imagery of v 11 and v 20). In the words of Jesus, "Out of the abundance of the heart the mouth speaks" (Matthew 12:34).

- **What does this suggest about how we can become less foolish with our words? What will (and what won't) "work"?** Here is the point at which the proverbs can be either misused or used well. The tendency, when applying proverbs, is to clench my jaw and resolve to do what they say. And of course, I will fail. I will fail if I try to apply the moral like a whip, either to myself or others. The key is fearing the Lord, living in relationship with him, reverencing him for who he is, and humbly listening to his words of life. The key is having the kind of heart, first of all, that receives God's word. Our words are just the outflow.

EXPLORE MORE
How does [James 3:1-12] reiterate what we've seen in Proverbs 10? What extra layers of meaning does it offer? As in Proverbs 10, James speaks of the tongue in violent terms. It is small but destructive! He also speaks to the source of our words— they "pour forth" from what's inside us (v 11). If we've been changed internally by

the Spirit, we "ought not" to curse others with our words (v 10).

How does Jesus solve the problem of our "salty spring" [John 4:13-14]? Change in our words is possible, because change in our hearts is possible, through Christ, by the power of the Spirit. Jesus said, "Out of the abundance of the heart the mouth speaks" (Matthew 12:34), and he promised to give water that will become in us a spring of water welling up to eternal life.

9. APPLY: How is Proverbs 10's wisdom on words different from the way in which the world normally encourages us to use words? How quick we are in our culture to speak, to "babble," and in fact to hold on to evil thoughts or intentions behind our words. Few around us are telling us to restrain our words. On the contrary, we are encouraged on all sides to speak and write all that we think and feel and do—in fact, to post the words so that hundreds or thousands can read them. Yet everyone recognizes that our words are somehow out of control. They so often don't bring refreshment or life to others; often they hurt.

10. APPLY: How have you seen the truth of Proverbs' teaching on words play out in your experience, both positively and negatively? As far as they are willing, encourage your group to share examples of the damage they have caused through foolish words. Also seek to draw out stories of how people have won victories in "taming the tongue" as they've walked with Jesus—or how they have seen words bring encouragement and life.

11. APPLY: Pick any one proverb from Proverbs 10 that you'd like to "chew" on this week. Why that one? This study has largely focused on the theme of words in Proverbs 10, but there are many other gems in this chapter! This final question is an opportunity for your group to talk about any of the proverbs which feel particularly pertinent to them. To help people keep "chewing" over the days ahead, you could provide post-it notes so that they can write down a relevant verse and stick it somewhere they'll see throughout the week.

NOTE: Our next study will pick up in chapter 14. Encourage your group to read Proverbs 11 – 13 at home before then.

5 Proverbs 14:1 – 16:9
THE LORD AT THE CENTER

BIG IDEA
The two ways of wisdom and folly are manifested in our emotional responses to others, our treatment of the poor, and ultimately our heart attitude toward the Lord.

SUMMARY
16:1-9 is the midpoint of "The Proverbs of Solomon"—and it turns out to be a significant midpoint indeed.

We'll first examine chapters 14 – 15 to see the themes growing there. Using mainly antithetic parallelism, the proverbs so far have consistently observed direct contrasts between the ways of wisdom and folly. That contrast goes by various names ("righteousness" vs. "wickedness," for example), but the fundamental difference is the one explained from the book's start: the way of wisdom is the way of one who fears the Lord and listens to his word; the way of folly is the way of one who despises the Lord and his instruction. Chapter 14 opens with a striking picture of the two ways. As in chapter 9, two women picture the two ways, making vivid the alternative paths available to every human being. Proverbs 14:2 explains the two ways one more time: the one walking in uprightness fears the Lord and the "devious" person despises him. The crux is one's attitude of heart toward the Lord God.

This attitude is manifested in the way one "walks" or lives. In this study we'll look particularly at the themes of anger (reckless words vs. restraint) and justice (oppression of the poor vs. generosity).

Toward the end of chapter 15 and into the first part of chapter 16 we arrive at a concentration of references to Yahweh, the Lord. The commentator Lindsay Wilson calls this section a "theological seam in the middle" of Solomon's proverbs (*Proverbs*, page 22). 16:1 and 9 form matching bookends, each beginning with the heart of a man that lays his plans, and each setting alongside those plans the Lord's final word (v 1b) or final direction (v 9b). 16:1-9 invites us to follow what we might call a "gospel train of thought": we are called to trust the sovereign Lord God (v 1-3); we are confronted with our sin and the punishment we deserve (v 4-5); we find atonement for that sin in God's steadfast love and faithfulness (v 6); and finally, we walk in relationship with him (v 7-9).

This is, obviously, the gospel still veiled in its Old Testament context, before all God's promises of steadfast love were revealed in Christ. And yet it is gospel truth, grounded in those promises and in the character of the Lord, who is the same yesterday, today, and forever.

OPTIONAL EXTRA

This study will include the famous instruction to "commit your work to the Lord" (16:8), which, as we'll see in question 8, has the sense of "rolling." To bring this to life and make it more memorable, have a ball ready to pass around the group. Rolling the ball into someone else's hands means that I have to let go myself!

GUIDANCE FOR QUESTIONS

1. "There is no black and white—there are only shades of gray." So goes a popular saying. From what you've read so far, would the writer of Proverbs agree? What makes you say that? The writer of Proverbs would probably say no! Using antithetic parallelism, the proverbs so far have consistently observed direct contrasts between the ways of wisdom and folly. This works out in a variety of similarly stark this-or-that contrasts: honest dealings vs. dishonest ones, truthful words vs. lies, and so on (as we saw in the previous study). These chapters will show us even more such contrasts. However, your group may observe that in real life there do indeed seem to be many shades of gray! Proverbs uses these different examples to keep drawing us back to the fundamental difference explained from the book's start: the way of wisdom is the way of one who fears the Lord and listens to his word; the way of folly is the way of one who despises the Lord and his instruction. On judgment day there will be no shades of gray but only black and white. That is not to say that, until then, some situations are not deceptive or that people are not complicated—we'll see in this study that Proverbs affirms both of those realities too (see questions 5 and 6).

2. How does 14:1 picture the two ways of wisdom and folly? The picture is of two women: one building a house, the other tearing it down. Wisdom's house in chapter 9 was a place of abundant life, with a feast laid out by Wisdom's own hands. In chapter 14 the picture is again of a *house*: a place where you *live* and share life with others. The contrasting foolish woman is not tearing down a literal physical house, but rather the life-filled connections with the people around her. "With her own hands" graphically lays the responsibility on this woman who breaks relationships; such was the "forbidden woman" of chapters 1 – 9, "who forsakes the companion of her youth and forgets the covenant of her God" (see 2:16-19). That woman's house was described as sinking down to death; in other words, she tore it down with her own hands. The two women point toward the ways in which we can build up or tear down the stability of the lives around us, creating either a safe, life-giving place or else a place of destruction, where the life is sucked out of the people we touch.

• **How does verse 2 describe the two ways? What is the crux of the difference?** Proverbs 14:2 pictures the upright person walking in fear of the Lord and the "devious" person despising him. As we've already seen in Proverbs, the crux of the difference between wisdom and folly is one's attitude of heart toward the Lord God.

3. What do the two ways look like in terms of a person's reactions? (14:16-19, 29; 15:18) The two ways look like recklessness vs. restraint. The temper which flares up again and again is an unmistakable marker of folly's path. The understanding person is "slow to anger," but the one with a "hasty temper exalts folly" (v 29).

4. What do the two ways look like in terms of a person's attitude to the poor (14:20-21, 31), and to wealth in general (15:16-17, 25)? These chapters develop a clear concern for justice in relation to the "poor," simply defined in these contexts as people who don't have enough to meet their material needs. 14:20 makes a sad but often true observation. In the next verse comes wisdom's perspective (14:21), which gets to the heart. The two ways are generosity vs. oppression.

• **Why is it wrong to oppress the poor?** This is our Father's world, and every human being in it is made in God's image, marred though that image has become by the fall. To oppress any human, then, is to insult that person's Maker, the Lord God, whereas (by contrast) to be generous to one in need honors the Lord, showing care for all he has made. This is no abstract law; how we treat what (or who) he has made is a very personal matter to God. In 15:25, the Lord himself is named as the one acting on behalf of justice. He wants his people to do the same.

EXPLORE MORE
How did God command his people to care for the poor [in Deuteronomy 15:7-15]? These verses explain in detail that if one of God's people should become poor in the land God was giving them, God's people were commanded not to harden their hearts or shut their hands, but rather: "You shall open wide your hand to your brother, to the needy and to the poor, in your land" (Deuteronomy 15:11).
Why were they to treat others this way (v 14-15)? The context for all their

generosity was God's repeated reminder of what he had done for them in rescuing them from slavery (v 15). Moreover, a poor Israelite was their "brother" (v 7)—implying a responsibility to care for one another. **How does this principle translate for Christians today? (See, for example, 2 Corinthians 9:6-15)** Christians today have likewise been redeemed from slavery to sin, at the cost of the life of God's Son. We have been united into the family of the church, and therefore likewise share a responsibility to care for our brothers and sisters who are struggling financially. In 2 Corinthians Paul appeals to the believers in Corinth to send a gift to help the believers in famine-stricken Jerusalem. Obedience would be an outworking of their "confession of the gospel of Christ" (2 Corinthians 9:13), and their generosity would be a mark of God's grace in their lives (v 14).

5. The two ways are not always easily discernible. Sometimes folly can masquerade as wisdom. Consider the following verses. How does the thing that appears better actually turn out to not be better at all?

- **14:4:** This verse warns us not to be deceived by the pleasing appearance of a clean barn. That means there's no hard work or productive labor going on, which would involve mud and sweat and dirty beasts!

- **15:17:** A dinner of a fattened ox would be a rich person's feast; it would appear to be the much better meal. But no matter how good the food is, when there are harsh words or underlying tensions, you are sure to lose your appetite.

- **Can you think of other examples, from your own life, where following wisdom's path looked worse on the surface but actually turned out to be better?** Allow your group to exchange ideas. I can't help but transfer 14:4 to the way many of us so often want our houses always to appear neat and clean—which sometimes means we've pushed to the side important relational "work" in which we, for example, allow the kitchen to get messed up by various helping hands, or we just don't mind if people see us in the midst of ongoing projects or games or whatever! There are better things than a clean manger.

6. What do these proverbs say about the heart (14:10, 13; 15:11, 13)? Do these verses ring true in your experience? These proverbs seem to stop and just look, with a kind of truthful compassion, into the human heart. 14:10 makes the observation that no person around you knows just what it's like to experience the particular bitternesses and joys you carry in your heart. Proverbs' wisdom sees and says it from all angles, reflecting the complexities of our human reality. Yes, "a glad heart makes a cheerful face," and by contrast a sorrowful heart crushes the spirit (15:13). Then again, the outward evidence doesn't always tell the full story (14:13). In 15:11 "Sheol" and "Abaddon" refer to the realms of death and destruction: the dark places we human beings imagine and fear. They are closed off to us; they lie open only before the Lord—which makes us think not only of his sovereign knowledge but also of his sovereign judgment. The parallelism here shows "hearts" lying open "before the Lord"—which makes us think of the same divine qualities in relation to our deepest thoughts and desires.

7. APPLY: Think about the different themes we've seen so far. How does

what you've read challenge the way you think about yourself, other people, and the Lord? A few points are offered below to stimulate your ideas, but the aim of this question is to allow your group to share whatever it is that has challenged them personally.

- **Anger:** It's easy to recognize anger in another person, and to realize its harm as we hear harsh words wielded like weapons or witness harsh actions that hurt deeply. It's also especially easy to justify our own anger, not seeing it with the eyes of others and feeling only the self-satisfying rush of emotion with which anger feeds us. Angry people are puffed up by the violence of their feelings; it's impossible to be humbly fearing the Lord and giving oneself to unrestrained anger at the same time.

- **Wealth and justice:** The principles of generosity and justice for the poor stand firm on the foundation of God the Creator. This alone would be enough to demand justice of us today. Yet when we think of all the further depths of revelation, culminating in God's great gift of salvation to us in his Son, how much more should our generosity overflow in thankful and merciful response!

- **The heart:** These verses guard against too easy assumptions concerning the people around us—particularly against assuming that we can understand what others are going through. We can't. But wonderfully, the Lord can.

8. Find the one command in these verses [Proverbs 16:1-9]. What does this mean, do you think? The one command comes in verse 3: "Commit your work to the LORD". The verb "commit" means literally to "roll" (Derek Kidner, *Proverbs*, page 118). Proverbs calls us to the ultimately humble

action of rolling our work (all our efforts) into the hands of the Lord—trusting him to "establish" our plans according to his sovereign plan. Rolling something into someone else's hands (picture a ball) means that I have to let go. This doesn't mean that I don't work hard and lay plans; it does mean that I actively give that work and those plans into the hands of the Lord.

- **Why can we have confidence as we do that, according to verses 1-2? (See also verse 9.)** Because the Lord is sovereign. 16:1 and 9 form matching bookends, each beginning with the heart of a man who lays his plans, and each setting alongside those plans the Lord's final word (v 1b) or final direction (v 9b). Verse 2 reiterates the idea of God's sovereignty, this time in his supreme knowledge of us his creatures. It is in light of this sovereign Lord that we are told to commit our work to him. What I commit to him might be a gathering I organized, or a career I planned, or a marriage or family I envisioned a certain way. God's way is often not what we envisioned. And yet, walking in relationship with him, fearing him, we find the path opening ahead of us, step by step.

9. What do verses 4-6 tell us about the problem of sin, and its solution? Three truths about sin emerge clearly. First, sin is not outside of God's sovereign control (16:4). This does not mean that God is the author of sin, but it does mean that he is sovereign over it and that his purposes prevail through it. Second, sin will be punished (16:5). Notice that it's not an evil action receiving punishment here, but rather an evil heart. If the arrogant in heart look like they're prospering now, don't worry, says Proverbs; punishment will surely come (although that punishment is not defined here). The third truth is that sin is atoned for in a certain way (16:6). "Steadfast love" and "faithfulness" are the words repeatedly used to describe the Lord's own covenant love for his people in the Old Testament (see, for example, Exodus 34:6; Numbers 14:18-19; Psalm 33:18-22). It is indeed through the Lord's steadfast love for his people that he mercifully provided a way for their sins to be forgiven and atoned for. For centuries this was through the system of temple sacrifices, but ultimately it was through the one perfect sacrifice of the Lord Jesus, to which all those other sacrifices pointed.

10. What are the blessings that come from a righteous life (that is, a life lived in the fear of the Lord) (v 7-9)? Here we read the final stage in the "gospel train of thought" of Proverbs 16:1-9 (see Summary above): walking in relationship with God. Verses 7-9 exude the blessings of a righteous life: that is, a life lived in the fear of the Lord. This person actually pleases the Lord and lives in peace (v 7). Even if such God-fearers are not materially rich, their little with righteousness is better than "great revenues with injustice" (v 8). When we finally come to verse 9, we read those words with increased confidence and insight. We have been confronted again with our need and with God's provision through his steadfast love and faithfulness. And so we will be quicker to commit our way to him—to roll our very lives into his sovereign hands.

EXPLORE MORE
Read Acts 4:23-31. How do these believers show us what it looks like to live out the truths of Proverbs 16:1-9? The believers acknowledge that God is the "sovereign Lord" (Acts 4:24), who establishes his plans, and they commit their work to him in prayer. They affirm that Herod and Pontius Pilate and others had gathered against Jesus "to do whatever your hand and your plan had predestined to take place" (Acts 4:24-28, compare Proverbs 16:4). And while the church's enemies in Acts do not make peace with them (as in Proverbs 16:7; remember, Proverbs gives principles, not promises), God certainly blesses them in other ways—filling them with his Holy Spirit and causing the church to bear fruit.

11. APPLY: What truths about the Lord in Proverbs 16:1-9 give you comfort and joy? How do those truths point you to Christ? Allow your group to share what has particularly struck them. Proverbs 16:6 points us beautifully to Christ. Through the blood of Jesus, the sinless Son of God, our sin was atoned for completely (Romans 3:22b-26; Hebrews 10:12-14). When we by faith trust in Christ for the forgiveness of our sins, we are experiencing the full and final meaning of Proverbs 16:6.

12. APPLY: Was there a particular time when you learned more of what it means that our hearts make our plans, but the Lord establishes our steps?
• How does that give you confidence as you look ahead to particular challenges you face in the future?
Encourage your group to share their stories, but be ready to step in with one of your own if necessary. Reflecting on how God has "come through" for us in the past encourages us to have confidence that he will do so again, whatever we face.

NOTE: The next study is on Proverbs 22:17 – 24:22. Therefore, you may want to encourage your group to read 16:10 – 22:16 at home before you next meet.

6 Proverbs 22:17 – 24:22
THIRTY SAYINGS OF THE WISE

BIG IDEA

Wise living flows from the desires of a heart that fears the Lord. Proverbs turns us away from chasing wealth or sensual over-indulgence, and towards the true strength of wisdom.

SUMMARY

A new collection is introduced in Proverbs 22:17: "The Words of the Wise." Many of these proverbs are closely related to an earlier Egyptian wisdom collection titled "Instructions of Amenemope"; evidence suggests that Solomon (or wise men under Solomon's direction) may have borrowed and adapted sections from this Egyptian source (Wilson, *Proverbs*, p 4). The adaptation grounds this wisdom in the fear of the Lord, shaping general revelation, which is accessible to all, into specific revelation, which is made alive by the breath of God. This dynamic between God-inspired and non-biblical writings is explored in the Explore More on page 35.

This section begins with a call to hear (Proverbs 22:17-21), similar to the father's calls in Proverbs 1 – 9. In this call the speaker and addressee are not identified, although the subsequent repetition of "my son" (23:15, 19, 26; 24:21) implies a setting similar to the earlier instructions.

For the purposes of this study, our journey through the Thirty Sayings of the Wise will focus around four key themes that we see repeated throughout Proverbs, and to which we now have the opportunity to turn our attention.

1) The folly of pursuing wealth and the wisdom of defending the poor (22:22 – 23:10). What most recognize as the first ten sayings in this collection begin and end with a defense of the poor and vulnerable: 22:22-23 and 23:10-11 give matching commands (not to take advantage of the poor) and reasons (because the Lord will plead their cause). Many of these examples relate to matters of civic justice. Within this section we find three sub-sections that also relate to wealth and poverty—this time in more private settings (23:1-8). Between two "dinner scenes" comes the lesson to be learned: wisdom's discernment in matters of wealth (v 4-5).

2) The relationship between parents and children (23:12-35). The focus in this section is on the *heart*: the father pours out his heart and pleads for the heart of his son (v 12, 15, 17). We'll note the need for loving discipline and instruction from parents to their children, and the call for children (even grown ones) to respect their parents (v 22-25).

3) Drunkenness and gluttony. The two evils most specifically targeted by the father in these passages are gluttony and drunkenness (v 19-21). Both represent a lack of restraint and an improper desire. To warn against drunkenness, this section includes a remarkable passage (v 29-35) that doesn't just argue the evil of too much alcohol; it takes us into the very experience of drunkenness. It dizzies us, perhaps makes us laugh (momentarily), and thoroughly impresses us with the deadly dangers of drunkenness.

4) The strength of wisdom in adversity (24:1-22). The final section of the "Words of the Wise" exalts wisdom's goodness and strength. *In contrast to envying the wicked* (v 1-2), Proverbs is saying, *this is what your heart should seek.* The opening verses picture wisdom's house (v 3-4), and the passage goes on to describe "a wise man"; he lives in the house and reflects its stability and goodness. Followers of the Lord likewise get to live in that house full of knowledge and understanding, from which we can emerge fully equipped for the "day of adversity" (v 10). There will indeed be days of adversity. But, as verse 16 says, "the righteous falls seven times and rises again."

OPTIONAL EXTRA

To stimulate your discussion in question 1, find a couple of commercials on YouTube to show to your group and then discuss. Themes relevant to this study would be commercials for luxury goods or vacations, scenes that depict the "ideal" family life or reflect typical aspirations for one's children, and ads for food and drink.

GUIDANCE FOR QUESTIONS

1. Think about some of the ads or commercials you've seen recently. What do they tell you about the kinds of things that people most desire? This question is intended to get your group thinking about the kinds of things that people in general (and they in particular) desire. Depending on the commercials that your group have seen recently, themes are likely to include wealth, luxury, status, comfort, approval, and pleasure. These will all stand in contrast to the wisdom that this passage tells us to desire!

EXPLORE MORE

How did the queen of Sheba respond to Solomon's wisdom [in 1 Kings 10:1-10]? Solomon's wisdom took her breath away (v 5)! She affirmed its truth and its benefits (v 6-8).

What did she recognize about Solomon (v 9)? She recognized that Solomon was set on the throne by the Lord, who evidently loved Israel and enabled Solomon to rule with justice and righteousness. She saw through his wisdom to his Lord.

Think about some of the wisdom that we've seen so far in Proverbs. How could you use that to connect with non-Christians you know, while pointing them to the source of true wisdom? Whether it's Proverbs' observations about the power of words or its recognition of the complexities of the human heart, we've seen time and again that this book's wisdom has the ring of truth to it. And it speaks into everyday experiences—natural things to talk to our friends and family about. You might challenge your group to start a conversation along the lines of: "I was reading in the Bible recently that _____. Does that ring true in your experience?" Perhaps talking about wisdom and the source of it will "take their breath away"—and give them a glimpse of the Lord Jesus.

2. Look at 22:22-23 and 23:10-11. How should the wise treat the poor, and why? 22:22-23 and 23:10-11 are bookends which give matching commands and reasons. First, do not rob the poor or crush the afflicted at the gate (22:22) because "the Lord will plead their cause" (v 23). And then in 23:10, "do not move an ancient landmark" (probably to take land from the poor) "or enter the fields of the fatherless" (probably to steal from the vulnerable)—for exactly the same reason (v 11). "Redeemer" is a word used many times in the Old Testament for God himself—as is surely the case here, especially in light of 22:23. Many of these examples relate to matters of civic justice: "the gate" in Proverbs 22:22 would be the entrance to a city where elders decided contentious matters; it was their courtroom. The "ancient landmarks" (23:10; see 22:28) were not just expressions of tradition; they marked God's sovereign distribution of the promised land to the tribes of Israel, as recorded in the law (Deuteronomy 19:14; 27:17). These proverbs address not just private oppression but also the political sorts of corruption that enable it, especially when those with power rule selfishly over those with none.

3. Why is the son warned to watch out…
- **in the house of the ruler (v 1-3)?** In both scenes, the son is called to restrain his appetite and to see through deception to discern the truth. The ruler's "deceptive food" (v 3) is perhaps to test or obligate him in some way, or maybe he's simply being warned that the delicacies of wealth can themselves become an entrapment—such a serious one that he should put a knife to his throat if he is "given to appetite" (v 2).

- **in the house of the stingy man (v 6-9)?** The stingy man's deception is his hypocrisy: he seems hospitable, with hearty-sounding invitations to eat and drink, but "his heart is not with you" (v 7). The son will later "vomit up the morsels" he's eaten, realizing the deception and the waste of his pleasant words on an evil man (v 8). Verse 9 may be taken as part of this sub-section, as it advises, "Do not speak in the hearing of a fool," who will despise words of good sense.

4. Between these two dinner scenes is the key lesson to be learned. What is

it (v 4-5)? The lesson is about wisdom's discernment in matters of wealth. It's a lovely passage: "Do not toil to acquire wealth; be discerning enough to desist. When your eyes light on it, it is gone, for suddenly it sprouts wings, flying like an eagle toward heaven" (v 4-5).

- **Why is toiling to acquire wealth foolish (v 5)?** Although wealth is often the reward of the wise in Proverbs, it is never a prize to be grasped for or toiled for. The memorable image shows the folly of such misplaced desire—as wealth sprouts wings and flies away like an eagle. This passage is about our heart's desire, which can so easily be captured by things that will pass away.

5. APPLY: Elsewhere Proverbs speaks of wealth as the reward of hard work, and warns that laziness leads to poverty. What are some differences between working hard to make a living and toiling to acquire wealth? How can we tell if we are being unwise in this area?
It is not easy to tell the difference! This is another area where we need wisdom's discernment. Questions to think about include: What are our goals? What do we daydream about having or owning or doing? Can we tell the difference between necessities and "nice-to-have's"? What is it that motivates us to get out of bed in the morning? Are we seeking to be diligent for the Lord's sake or for wealth's sake? Would we ever say no to the opportunity to make more money, if we already had enough? In the end, is our heart's desire to please the Lord, no matter what?

6. APPLY: Who are the poor or defenseless near you, whose cause you could plead? How could you seek to light up their lives with God's justice

and mercy? Gates and ancient landmarks don't directly apply to us today. What does apply is God's clear message that he cares for and will defend the poor and vulnerable—and that to be wise is to be like him in this regard. In these proverbs the Lord is not pictured as standing back and responding to this or that; he is active, proactive, stepping forward to "plead the cause" of the defenseless and punish those who harm them. Our particular context will guide what this needs to mean for us. One unavoidable subject in this regard is surely abortion. A pregnant woman is vulnerable, and the baby in her womb is utterly defenseless. We cannot escape being complicit in this issue, which connects to the people and the power of the societies and the communities in which we live (consider also the warning in Proverbs 24:11-12).

7. What do these verses [Proverbs 23:12-35] say about...

• **how parents should relate to their children?** The father pours out his heart and pleads for the heart of his son (v 12, 15, 17). In these warm, affectionate verses, the father obviously yearns for the good of his child. It is in this context that verses 13-14 urge discipline, in this case even the striking of a child with a rod—which will not kill him but might "save his soul from Sheol." Whatever specific stance we might take on corporal discipline, the clear principle is that children need discipline—both instruction in good ways and consequences for bad ways (but always, as in these verses, in the context of love). We live in a fallen world, with folly bound up in the heart of each one of us (see 22:15). Hence the importance of teaching God's word to young people so that they can hear early in life and "direct [their] hearts" in

the way of wisdom (23:19). Of course, such views are utterly contrary to many of the assumptions around us today: that children are by nature good; that they should be allowed to find their own way according to their natural desires; that rules and discipline constrict rather than enable. Proverbs urges us to see these ideas for what they are: foolish!

• **how children should relate to their parents?** Verses 22-25 highlight the relationship of the son to his parents, who are instructing him. These verses echo the call of the fifth commandment: to "honor" your father and your mother (Exodus 20:12). Why? It's not just because they're wise; it's that your father "gave you life" (Proverbs 23:22) and your mother "bore you" (v 25). And it's not just so as to obey the commandment; it's also so that your parents will "greatly rejoice" and be "glad" in their child (v 24-25; see 10:1). This is beautiful—but hard for children to do! The force of sin's pull to disobey is strong (see again 22:15). 23:22 also implies that there exists a temptation to "despise" (scorn, or at least stop honoring) aged parents. Elderly parents become increasingly slow and weak; it takes effort for adult children to make their parents a part of their lives. Energetic grandchildren and great-grandchildren likewise have to be taught to stop and converse with them thoughtfully. There is a lot to think on and work on here!

8. What two specific evils does the father warn his son against (v 19-21, 29-35)? Gluttony and drunkenness. These are sins that often go together and that are put together, twice, in verses 20-21. (We often scold about drunkenness while forgetting to note the evil of gluttony.)

• **What do these things have in common? What makes them so dangerous? And how do these verses powerfully communicate the danger?** Both represent a lack of restraint and an improper desire; so, in these verses, the dire consequences of poverty and rags are applied to both together. Proverbs is not speaking to whether or when we should consume alcohol. What is described in 23:29-35 is the self-destructive folly of over-consumption. (Spend some time taking in the pictures in this passage.) Most of us will know someone whose life has been destroyed by the deadly effects of alcohol or drugs. These dangers are not new. From generation to generation, people with godly sense must pass on these warnings, embedding them in loving instruction that turns hearts toward knowing and fearing the Lord.

9. Looking at [24:3-18], why is wisdom much more desirable instead [of envying the wicked]? Verses 3-4 take us back to Proverbs 9, with Wisdom building her house, preparing her feast, and calling us in. This house is a picture not only of where we should live but of where we should most want to live—in the Lord's presence. In contrast to envying the wicked, Proverbs is saying, this is what your heart should seek. Verse 5 emphasizes the wise man's "strength" and "might," referring not to his muscles but to his wisdom, and the wisdom of many through whose guidance wars are waged and victory is won (v 6). Verses 13-14 picture the sweet dripping of the honeycomb: "wisdom is such to your soul" (v 14a).

10. What hope do these verses offer for when we encounter hard times (v 5, 10, 16)? Most of us know what it is to feel "faint in the day of adversity" (v 10). Proverbs tells us where to look for strength of heart: to the Lord, whom we fear. "A wise man is full of strength" (v 5a). These verses can and should encourage us. Followers of the Lord get to live in that house full of knowledge and understanding, from which we can emerge fully equipped for hard times. There will indeed be days of adversity. But, as verse 16 says, "The righteous falls seven times and rises again." The wicked will stumble and fall (v 16-17), but the righteous are pictured as falling and rising, again and again—never defeated.

• **How will wise people respond when others encounter difficulties (v 17-18)?** Amid talk of war and victory and strength and the wicked falling, verses 17-18 stop us short if we are those who have a tendency to gloat over the fall of our rivals. Scripture shows plenty of righteous rejoicing in God's victories over his enemies, but we must beware a more personal sense of self-righteous revenge.

11. APPLY: In what areas have the thirty sayings of the wise shown your desires to be out of kilter? This study has taken in a broad range of themes: wealth, justice, family life, food and alcohol, and more. This question is an opportunity for members of your group to share which challenges have particularly struck them.

12. APPLY: We live in a world that encourages us to desire so much other than wisdom! As a community of believers, how can we help one another to remember that the Lord's wisdom is our ultimate source of goodness and strength? Encourage your group to share their ideas. Consider, for example, what you tend to talk about before your Bible study or after a Sunday service. Is Jesus Christ at the center of our thoughts and words? Our churches ought to be oases of respite from the constant bombardment of the world's "wisdom," yet so often the subject of our conversation reveals that we have largely the same aspirations—careers, vacations, home improvements, and academic achievement for our kids. So instead of asking, "How has

work been?" why not try "How has God been good to you this week?"

NOTE: The next study will pick up in Proverbs 30. Once again, you might like to encourage your group to read the intervening chapters (24:23 – 29:27) at home before you next meet.

7 Proverbs 30:1-33
A HUMBLE HEART

BIG IDEA

Wise living means receiving God's gifts with a humble heart, rather than seeking to exalt ourselves.

SUMMARY

Nobody knows who Agur is, yet he gives us the book of Proverbs' most personal account of what it's like to live out the fear of the Lord. We'll look at Agur's relationship with God (30:1-9), and then we'll hear his corresponding wise words about God's world (v 10-33). What we'll find, as we've found all along, is that the wise do not exalt themselves, but rather receive God's gifts with a humble heart.

In verses 2-3, with as much literary force as possible (using "hyperbole": that is, exaggeration to make a point), Agur shows that he understands how small his wisdom is, and how limited is his knowledge of the infinitely glorious "Holy One" (see 9:10). Then, after setting his own small store of human wisdom in perspective, Agur looks up and celebrates the God who gives wisdom to us, in his word (v 5-6). Proverbs 30:7-9 is the only prayer in the entire book. It completes this chapter's first section, in which we are

given a personal glimpse of someone who fears the Lord. When we get to questions 4 and 5, think about how Agur's requests show his humility. They could be summed up as the most basic of requests—those of a child: *Clean me and feed me.*

In the chapter's second part (v 10-33) it feels as if Agur gets up from his prayers and goes outside. As he does so, we observe the world through the eyes of a wise man with a humble heart. A brief overview is helpful. First, notice three key points at which a warning appears: verse 10 begins the chapter's second half with a somewhat subtle warning; verse 17 stops and gives a more dramatic warning; and verses 32-33 conclude with a warning that clarifies (and vividly illustrates) the main point of the section.

These key points hold together various lists of observations. Between verses 10 and 17 come *two lists*:

• Verses 11-14 list four arrogant kinds of people.
• Verses 15-16 list first two, and then three, no, *four* things that always want more.

Between verses 17 and 32 come *four lists*:

• Verses 18-20 list first four wonderful

things and then a terrible one.

- Verses 21-23 list four over-reachers.
- Verses 24-28 list four small wise things.
- Verses 29-31 list four "stately" things.

Humble Agur's intensive "organizing" here at the end of Proverbs highlights a wise ability to see into God's order, to delight in the seeing, and to communicate what it means to live (and not to live) according to God's ways.

OPTIONAL EXTRA

To help your group enter into Agur's sense of wonder in the natural world, you could show them some YouTube clips from nature documentaries: eagles, snakes, ants, rock badgers, locusts, lizards, lions… they're all praised in Proverbs 30! (Or, to convey the repulsion of verse 15, find a clip of leeches— if your group has strong enough stomachs!).

GUIDANCE FOR QUESTIONS

1. Most of us have a long list of prayer requests that we regularly pray about. But imagine you could only ask God for two things. What would they be, and why? Try to get people to be specific and to write something down. You will come back to these answers when you get to question 7.

2. We're nearing the end of a book that is intended to help us to "know wisdom" (1:1). What, then, is surprising about Agur's words in 30:1-3? We might expect someone at the end of this book to step up and say, "I've got it. I have learned wisdom." Instead Agur says he has not learned wisdom, and calls himself stupid and without human understanding.

- **Read Proverbs 26:12. What is not surprising about Agur's attitude?**
  26:12 shows us the ultimate folly of being

wise in one's own eyes (see also 26:5 and 26:16). Proverbs has continually and increasingly connected the fear of the Lord with a humble and not an arrogant heart (see, for example, 15:33; 16:5-6; 21:4; 22:4; 29:23). The prologue called the wise to "hear and increase in learning" (1:5; see 9:9). A truly wise person would never stop, look at himself, and say he has learned wisdom. With as much literary force as possible, Agur is showing that he understands how small is his wisdom and how limited his knowledge of the infinitely glorious "Holy One" (see 9:10).

3. What are the answers to Agur's questions in verse 4, humanly speaking? The most obvious answer is "No one." No person has done any of these things; how, then, could any of us ever think we are wise? The end is like a taunt: *Surely you know, all you who think you are wise!* But there is no such human father and son. That's the point.

- **What other answer could we give to those questions?** "God." The resonances with Job 38:1 – 40:5 are unmistakable here. This sense of awe and reverence before the Lord God, who created all things, is at the heart of the wisdom that Proverbs (and all the Bible's wisdom literature) teaches. Proverbs does not tell us the name of the son (Proverbs 30:4), but living this side of the incarnation, we do know the son's name: Jesus! Looking back, we see the mystery solved.

EXPLORE MORE
What similarities do you see between Proverbs 30:4 and Job 38:1-11? How does Job model a wise response to God's creative might (40:3-5)? The similarities should be obvious. Both passages cause us to marvel at God alone

as the sole Creator and Sustainer of the universe. No one and nothing compares to him. How foolish we are, then, to try to exalt ourselves! Job rightly admits his smallness (40:4); rather than seeking to speak, he is now content to listen.

4. Look at verse 5. Why are both halves of this verse important, and wonderful? How wonderful that it is not just Scripture's general meaning that is true, but that Scripture's every word is true, written by authors who were carried along by the Holy Spirit to write down exactly the words God intended (2 Peter 1:21). But we must not stop there; it is through the perfectly true word of God that we know him and take refuge in him. So these are not two unrelated lines. They are actually a great corrective to any of us who might tend to isolate line 1 and simply wax eloquent on its theological truth. The word "proves" in line 1 indicates a refining process: the truth of God's word is proven repeatedly; it shines out more and more brightly. To trust this word is to take refuge in him; he is our shield (see 20:22). This is personal truth.

5. Sum up what "two things" Agur asks God for in verses 7-9. In short, "clean me" and "feed me." The first request is this: "Remove far from me falsehood and lying" (v 8a). In the context of what we've just read (v 5-6), Agur is asking God to align his heart and his words with the truth of God's word: that he would not speak what God's word calls false; that he would not add to God's word; that he would not listen to or promote false voices around him that go against God's word. Agur's second request comes in two parts: "Give me neither poverty nor riches" (30:8b) and then "Feed me with the food that is needful for me" (v 8c). Verse 9 goes on to explain the risks that he perceives

in riches and poverty: risks relating not just to his own well-being but to his relationship with the Lord, and to the glory of the Lord's name. He is asking for whatever God knows he needs in order to walk according to God's word, glorifying his name.

6. What do Agur's prayer requests reveal about his attitude? Implicit in Agur's first request is his acknowledgment of his sin and weakness. He doesn't say, *Help me to believe and speak truth.* Rather, he asks God to remove falsehood far from him; he knows his tendency to fall back into it. Implicit also is Agur's trust in God's word as having proven true, and in God as his shield and refuge from evil. He knows his weakness, but he also knows the Lord who will deliver him. And so he asks. In his second request Agur is honest enough to admit that he is vulnerable to straying. In wealth, he might come to feel self-sufficient and deny or simply forget about the Lord; in poverty, he might steal and "profane the name of my God." We can learn much from the deep humility in this request, as it ultimately trusts God to know better than we do what we need.

7. APPLY: Compare Agur's prayer requests with your answer to question 1. What might you need to learn from him? Truthful words, and truth that resonates with God's word, might not be high on our list of requests—but maybe they should be. If at the end of each day we make it a practice to be quiet and simply think back through the words we have given out and taken in, we will have plenty to confess and plenty to pray about. We could sum up his prayer as *Clean me. Feed me.* That's humbling, because they're the two most basic needs of a little child. Maybe our prayers should go back to such basics.

- **How might your prayer times as a group sound different if you were to take a leaf out of Agur's book?** Bible-study group members often put together prayer lists, and they can get long. And that's not bad. It's encouraging to be able to share our requests, and to know brothers and sisters are praying—for our hearts, for loved ones, for challenges in health, finances, employment, and on and on. But Agur has just two things on his list. These are the two things he'll pray until he dies (v 7). He's a minimalist; he's getting down to the basics here. These two things help all of us see through to the most basic concerns that should guide our petitions to the Lord.

8. What do these proverbs [30:10-17] have to say about humility, self-exaltation, and grasping for more? This is not a straightforward question, so don't be afraid to give your group time to think and "chew." To slander someone else's servant (v 10) sounds like a pathetic attempt to raise oneself up by stepping on a person who is lowly and defenseless. The next four verses each appear to describe a category of people who are exalting themselves in wrongful ways: children cursing the parents they should honor (v 11); filthy unwashed people who are "clean in their own eyes" (v 12); people who raise their eyes and look down on everybody (v 13); and, finally, those who violently wipe out the poor and needy from off the earth (v 14). Verses 15-16 look into the natural world and find reflections of this same grasping for more—a grasping that is never satisfied. Capping these lists of graspers-for-more is one of the chapter's key points in 30:17. The mocking child here is arrogantly scorning the good pattern repeatedly celebrated in this book, elevating himself over the ones to whom he should humbly look and listen.

9. What is the common thread that ties together each of these "fours" [in Proverbs 30:18-33]? What is being celebrated, or condemned?
- **Verses 18-19, and 20.** Verses 18-19 celebrate order—with everything beautiful in its place, within its bounds (the very thing self-exaltation breaks down). It seems fitting that the final wonderful "thing" should be the coming together of a man and a woman in the sexual union of marriage. This goodness contrasts with the evil of verse 20, where the adulteress has taken her fill outside of marriage.

- **Verses 21-23.** This is a negative list of overreachers—four instances of people in one way or another wrongly changing status. These verses seem to describe the rewarding of people who are not wise. It is helpful to remember that the history of Israel is a history of the lowly being raised; the recurring pattern of God's working is that humility comes before honor.

- **Verses 24-28.** These are "small" things, "but they are exceedingly wise" (v 24). What is the nature of their wisdom? Each is limited, but alongside these limitations are corresponding and remarkable positives. These "wise" small creatures are living *with the grain* of the created order, not *against the grain*—living, we might say, in submission to their Creator. Through his observations about the natural world, Agur is speaking into human experience; he is recommending the lowly way, the way of humility—which is the way of wisdom, grounded in the fear of the Lord.

- **Verses 29-31.** The final list offers four things that walk with dignity and confidence. In contrast to the lowly creatures we've just seen, these creatures seem to have been given a kind of innate "highness"—except, that is, the king, who joins this list as "stately" only when his army is with him (v 31b). Perhaps there is a warning here for imperfect kings who might be tempted to strut like roosters but who left alone might turn tail and run!

10. In what sense do verses 32-33 sum up the message of chapter 30?
• What is the alternative to "exalting yourself" (v 32), according to Proverbs?
Here, again, is a call to humility. In the context of the whole chapter (and of the book), it's a call to fear the Lord, listening to his word and walking humbly in his ways. Agur would say the Lord's "way" is too wonderful for him; he does not understand it. And yet, in his humility, he has begun to understand it, and he has communicated it to us in ways that penetrate our imaginations and our hearts. This is the alternative to "exalting yourself." The final three pictures of Proverbs 30:33 are of the results of various kinds of "pressing"—and so we are warned, with the most down-to-earth pictures, of the results of self-exaltation.

11. APPLY: How does the culture around us encourage us not to be humble and lowly? Our culture encourages us to climb to the top of the career ladder; to throw off tradition and societal expectations and "be true to yourself"; to laud our achievements and connections on social media; to "never apologize, never explain." Advertising encourages us to grasp for more and more material possessions and expensive experiences as the way to be happy and fulfilled. What contrasts to Agur's proverbs

encouraging us to embrace God's created order, to admit our sin, need, and weakness, and to live in fear of the Lord!

• How might our church culture encourage us not to be humble?
Often, in all the same ways as above—but perhaps with a thin religious veneer. Or, for example, it may be that "up front" gifts are more readily celebrated and valued than lowly, behind-the-scenes tasks.

12. APPLY: How does Jesus show us the way of humility, which leads to honor (Philippians 2:6-11)? How does he enable us to follow him in that way?
Our Lord Jesus showed fully to us the way of humility (i.e. the way of wisdom) when he made himself nothing, taking the form of a servant, being born in the likeness of men—humbling himself by becoming obedient to the point of death, even death on a cross (Philippians 2:7-8). But he rose from the grave, having accomplished the work of our salvation, and ascended into heaven, our risen and eternal King. Jesus, our wisdom from God, shows us wisdom's way of humility, which leads to honor.

• What should humility look like in our treatment of others (v 1-5)? Our humility should shine forth in our unity and love, in a lack of selfish ambition or conceit, and in the way that we put the interests of others before our own. Encourage your group to identify some specific ways in which they could live out this humble, Christ-like love in your church.

8 Proverbs 31:1-31
WISDOM LIVED

BIG IDEA

Wise living is strong and beautiful. We who fear the Lord will be blessed in lives of wholehearted work, as we humbly serve those around us, trusting in the Lord to the end.

SUMMARY

The final chapter of Proverbs contains first another oracle, and then the famous epilogue to the book: the poem about the "excellent wife." After briefly looking at this short oracle, we'll give the bulk of our attention in this study to the book's epilogue, letting it help us to conclude this discussion of the book of Proverbs.

Proverbs 31:1-9: These verses deliver another oracle of another man unknown to us (see 30:1)—except that he is a king. This is King Lemuel speaking, but we're told that he's quoting words his mother taught him. How lovely to see, here at the end, a son who listened and learned. And how encouraging, after seeing a mother *not* blessed (30:11) and a mother *scorned* (30:17), to find a mother honored by her son. The oracle gives a negative command and a related positive command. The negative command: kings must not give themselves to women and alcohol, lest they forget their duty to defend the rights of the afflicted (31:2-5). The positive command: defend the rights of the afflicted (v 6-9).

Proverbs 31:10-31: It seems utterly appropriate that Proverbs should end with a woman, after all the female figures we've met in the previous 30 chapters. Proverbs 31 is a picture of a real-life woman (not a personification of wisdom). In the book's

context, it is written not to women but to men, to give a portrait of the wife a man should seek and celebrate. However, in the largest context, it gives to all of us readers a final portrait of wisdom in action—the wisdom we all should seek.

This poem is Proverbs' finale in a number of ways, not least in its poetic intricacy and excellence. It is written as an acrostic: the twenty-two verses begin consecutively with the twenty-two letters of the Hebrew alphabet. Acrostic poems are like a puzzle with many pieces, sort of like the book of Proverbs itself. But this poem does have discernible sections. The introduction (v 11-12) sets forth this excellent wife; the main body of the poem (v 13-27) shows her in action; the conclusion (v 28-31) steps back and lets us hear praise resounding in her honor.

Structural markers help: the word "excellent" appears in verse 10 and then in verse 29, bookending the poem. The husband in particular plays a key part in the poem's structure, appearing at the beginning (v 11-12); in the middle (v 23); and at the end (v 28-29). This wife is given to us in relation to her husband; that is the context in which this woman fits and where she thrives.

The wife's foundational relationship with the Lord is mentioned only at the poem's end (31:30). This climactic mention of the fear of the Lord provides a bookend not for this poem but rather for the book as a whole. The fear of the Lord was introduced as wisdom's foundation (1:7); it bookended Proverbs' first section (9:10); it served as a strong thread binding together the proverbs (for example, in 15:33 – 16:9); and now the fear of the Lord pulls together the entire book (31:30). For all its swirls of verses, Proverbs is a literary work with a remarkably coherent shape. The fear of the Lord holds it together.

Because the majority of the questions in this study look at Proverbs 31:10-31 as a whole, there is no natural halfway point at which to break the study into two sessions. However, if you wish to divide the study into two parts, you could finish your first study after question 5 by asking the optional application question in this Leader's Guide. Alternatively, if you know you will be pressed for time you could skip questions 2 and 3 (on verses 1-9) and focus your study on the book's epilogue.

OPTIONAL EXTRA

Proverbs 31:10-31 is an acrostic poem—what we in English might call the "A to Z of wisdom." To help your group review what they've learned from the book of Proverbs, write your own A to Z. Distribute the "letters" between your group members (with one person or pair doing A – D, the next doing E – H, and so on), and give them a few minutes to come up with a short phrase reflecting something they've learned about wisdom, beginning with each of those letters (e.g. *A*ll about the fear of the Lord. *B*eware the adulterous woman. *C*are for the poor). Come back together and read your A to Z aloud.

GUIDANCE FOR QUESTIONS

1. Imagine that a young unmarried man at your church asked you, "What should I look for in a wife?" How would you answer? The aim of this question is to help set the context of Proverbs 31:10-31 in people's minds—and to give an opportunity to clarify that this context expands to include all of us. Proverbs' perspective has consistently been that of a son receiving words of wisdom from a father or a wise speaker—including wisdom concerning which women to follow and which to avoid. The prologue lets us understand that we can all learn from this wisdom; we readers have shared the son's perspective, for all of us must learn to turn away from folly and follow the path of wisdom. Following the perspective of the book, then, Proverbs 31 is not written to women to instruct them in how to be good wives; it is written to men (and to all of us) to instruct them (and all of us) in what we should seek.

2. What are kings called to do [in Proverbs 31:1-9]? Lemuel's mother calls him to defend the poor and needy (Proverbs 31:9), who here include: the "afflicted" (v 5), "the one who is perishing" (v 6), "those in bitter distress" (v 6), those in poverty and misery (v 7), and the mute and the destitute (v 8). From his position of power, the king is to lift up these needy ones, opening his mouth to speak for them and to "judge righteously" on their behalf (v 8-9).

• **What behavior is not fitting for a king, and why?** Lemuel's mother pleads with him not to give his energy and focus to sinful excesses (in this case, with women and wine, v 3-4), which will disable him from fulfilling a true king's calling (v 5, see 23:29-35). Powerful rulers met these temptations in a powerful way; King Solomon himself desperately needed this wisdom (see 1 Kings 11:1-2).

3. How did Jesus fulfill the kingly calling in Proverbs 31:8-9? (See also Luke 7:22 and Isaiah 11:1-4.) Encourage your group to recall examples from the Gospels when Jesus acted for the good of the poor and needy (e.g. Luke 7:11-17, Mark 7:31-37).

These in turn point to his identity as the Messiah, God's anointed King, who came to raise up the spiritually poor by giving us his righteousness. When John the Baptist sent his messengers to Jesus to ask him if he was truly the promised Messiah (Luke 7:18-20), he replied affirming that he did indeed fulfill what was spoken about the Messiah in passages such as Isaiah 11:1-4.

4. How do verses 10-12 and 28-31 provide a framework for the poem? See notes on the structure in the "Summary" above.

• **Stand back and look at the big picture [of Proverbs 31:10-31]. What kind of words would you use to describe this woman?** Your group could legitimately choose any number of words! That said, perhaps one of them should be "strength." 31:10-31 is a strong poem celebrating a strong woman, and the very shape of the poem reflects her strength. The acrostic format sets forth solid building blocks that create a comprehensive and sturdy structure. The poem's main sections encase this woman securely in the relationships of her life, all in their proper places even as they expand before our eyes.

5. What kinds of work does she do, and in what manner? First, *the Proverbs 31 woman works hard.* She's the opposite of the sluggard. The book's theme of hard work and its rewards (versus laziness and its consequences) comes to completion in this woman, with verse after verse of busy productivity: making fine garments and textiles (Proverbs 31:13, 19, 22, 24); procuring and preparing food for her household (v 14, 15); buying property and planting vineyards (v 16); selling garments (v 24); and instructing others (v 26). Verse

27 sums it up well. Second, *the Proverbs 31 woman works willingly to serve those around her* (v 13b). She is not working simply for her own advancement and her own good. Her "household" is mentioned four times (v 15, 21 (twice), 27), and we will see her care for the poor and needy. Third, *this woman creatively makes things in her work.* Her mind is working as well; she "considers" (v 16) and "perceives" (v 18). This woman is, through her work, creating new things (v 19), imaging the Creator God. Proverbs tells us that hard work—willing, servant-like, creative work—will bring glory to our Creator and great good to all those around us.

⊻

• **What would it look like to go about your work in a more "Proverbs 31" manner this week? How does this chapter challenge and encourage you?**

6. How does this woman relate to...

• **her husband?** The enclosing structure of this poem—with the husband at the beginning (v 11-12), in the middle (v 23), and at the end (v 28-29)—shows that all this woman's work is done in the context of this marital relationship, and with the goal of doing her husband "good, and not harm" unceasingly, "all the days of her life" (v 12). This wife is embracing her wife-ship. We see that her work reaches far, but even in its farthest reach it is not unrelated to her relationship with her husband. He's right there in the center of the poem, sitting among the elders of the land (v 23). She is lifting him up with all her work, which is praised not just by her husband but also "in the gates" (v 31).

• **her household?** She works hard to

provide for her household (v 15, 21), including her "maidens" (that is, maidservants). Hers is clearly a well-to-do household, but not a stingy or ingrown one. She has the respect of her children: they "rise up and call her blessed" (v 28).

- **her community?** She is generous to the needy—not just opening her hand to give but reaching out her hands, plural (v 20), perhaps to give more, or perhaps to lift up or embrace a needy one. She knows the truth of Proverbs 14:31. And she is well respected—she is praised at the city gates, where the elders meet (v 31, 23).

- **her God?** More important than all this woman's human relationships is a relationship with her Maker; that is, with the Lord God. She fears the Lord (v 30). This is the source of her blessing, and this is what will last.

7. As the book's concluding piece, this poem draws together the themes of wisdom that we have seen throughout. For example, how do verses 10-11 specifically echo 3:13-14? The goal in both passages is to "find" (31:10; 3:13) this wife/wisdom, which is "more precious than jewels" (31:10; 3:15). The "gain from her" in 3:14 is echoed in 31:11. Clearly, this poem is not just about a wife; it is, in a larger sense, a final portrait of wisdom— wisdom lived out.

- **How does verse 26 resonate with what we've seen elsewhere in Proverbs?** For one thing, this woman is characterized more by her actions than by a lot of words, perhaps demonstrating the restraint that Proverbs advises (see 17:27). When this woman does speak, however, wisdom comes out, and "the teaching of kindness is on her tongue" (31:26). That word "teaching" comes from the Hebrew

torah, or law, and the word "kindness" from the Hebrew *hesed*, as in the Lord's steadfast love for his people. On this woman's tongue is the word and the love of God himself.

8. … this woman "fears the Lᴏʀᴅ." What is she *not* afraid of, and why (v 21, 25)? In verse 21 she does not entertain even the most common fears for the safety of her loved ones, for she has made them clothes of scarlet—meaning either clothes of fine fabric or clothes of double-thickness, which are extra warm. These are literal clothes, but they also create an impression of the spiritual richness and security of wisdom— which can be found in the poorest and simplest households, where only the Lord is feared. This joyful security is wonderfully communicated as this woman "laughs at the time to come" (31:25). This woman lives in relationship with the Lord, fearing him and following his word, and so she has confidence in the future, knowing her hope will never be "cut off" (23:18). It's not that she thinks bad things won't happen; she knows "the righteous falls seven times and rises again" (24:16).

EXPLORE MORE
Read Ruth 3:1-13. Think about what you know about Ruth from the book as a whole. What has she done that makes her an *eshet hayil*? What does she have in common with the Proverbs 31 woman? The widow Ruth has faithfully cared for her mother-in-law, Naomi, leaving behind her own land of Moab to return with Naomi to Bethlehem and declaring allegiance to the Lord God of Israel (Ruth 1:16). In Bethlehem, Ruth has worked humbly and hard in Boaz's fields, gleaning barley from morning till night (Ruth 2). This is one *eshet hayil*!

In what ways is her situation different to that of the Proverbs 31 woman? Even while resonating with the truths of Proverbs 31's *eshet hayil*, Ruth's strengths unfold quite differently. Ruth is a poor widow with no children, not a well-to-do wife with husband and children as is the woman of Proverbs 31.

How does this encourage you, as you seek to live out wisdom's strength in your own situation? Whatever our own circumstances—married or single, with children or without, male or female—it is possible to live out wisdom's strength! All of us can take to heart the lessons of Proverbs 31.

9. APPLY: Who do you know who embodies this Proverbs 31 wisdom? How do they spur you on to seek to live out wisdom? Be ready with your own example if your group are struggling. This should hopefully be a wonderful opportunity to honor some of the wise women (and men) in your congregation, while thinking about what these characteristics look like in the 21st century.

10. APPLY: How might this poem help you praise the Lord for "the depth of the riches and wisdom and knowledge of God" (Romans 11:33), all made known to us in Christ? This is an opportunity for your group to think about how Proverbs 31:10-31 shows the blessings of a life lived in Christ, our wisdom from God.

11. APPLY: How does Proverbs 31 excite you about living together as God's people in Christ? It is exciting that we believers live out this high calling of wisdom not individually but all together, uniting our gifts and our wholehearted work all for the glory of the One who laid down his life to redeem us. In this sense we might glimpse in this poem a picture of a church community that is busy about the work of looking after one another, blessing the needy and bringing honor to our "husband," the Lord Jesus.

12. APPLY: Look back over the previous studies. What has most thrilled, challenged, or encouraged you from your time in the book of Proverbs?

Dive deeper into Proverbs

In the Proverbs, God offers us wisdom for real life, and he shows us Jesus, who was wisdom personified and exemplified. This accessible, absorbing expository guide to Proverbs by Kathleen Nielson brings these ancient sayings to life, helping ordinary Christians to see what it can look like to enjoy living in line with God's wisdom in the great multitude of everyday situations and decisions we face. This book gives an expository rather than topical treatment to the book of Proverbs, so it can be read as originally intended. It also has more application than a typical commentary, making it a great resource for personal devotions as well as useful for leading small-group studies or sermon preparation.

thegoodbook
COMPANY

BIBLICAL | RELEVANT | ACCESSIBLE

At The Good Book Company, we are dedicated to helping Christians and local churches grow. We believe that God's growth process always starts with hearing clearly what he has said to us through his timeless word—the Bible.

Ever since we opened our doors in 1991, we have been striving to produce Bible-based resources that bring glory to God. We have grown to become an international provider of user-friendly resources to the Christian community, with believers of all backgrounds and denominations using our books, Bible studies, devotionals, evangelistic resources, and DVD-based courses.

We want to equip ordinary Christians to live for Christ day by day, and churches to grow in their knowledge of God, their love for one another, and the effectiveness of their outreach.

Call us for a discussion of your needs or visit one of our local websites for more information on the resources and services we provide.

Your friends at The Good Book Company